LOIRE
VALLEY
in your pocket

MAIN CONTRIBUTOR: JACK ALTMAN

PHOTOGRAPH CREDITS
Photos supplied by The Travel Library: 6, 12, 21, 33,
54, 59, 82, 107, 120; A Amsel 38, 56; John Mole front
cover, 8, 111; Rob Moore title page, 5, 10, 14, 17, 26,
27, 29, 32, 34, 40, 41, 42, 43, 45, 46, 48, 51, 52, 57, 58,
60-61, 62, 64, 66, 69, 70, 71, 72, 73, 74, 75, 76, 77, 80,
81, 83, 84, 85, 88, 89, 91, 95, 96, 99, 101, 104, 109,
113, 119, 123, 125, 126; R Richardson 30, 35, 36, 37,
49, 78, 86, 102; Clare Roberts 47, 55, 68, 87, 124;
Peter Terry 24; G Walden back cover, 53, 97.
Other photos: D Hodges 79; Natural Image/Bob
Gibbons 105.

*Front cover: Azay-le-Rideau; back cover: ornamental
gardens, Château Villandry; title page: detail of façade,
Maison d'Adam, Angers*

MANUFACTURE FRANÇAISE DES PNEUMATIQUES MICHELIN

Place des Carmes-Déchaux – 63000 Clermont-Ferrand (France)

© Michelin et Cie. Propriétaires-Éditeurs 1997

Dépôt légal Mai 97 – ISBN 2-06-630701-7 – ISSN 1272-1689

No part of this publication may be reproduced in any form

without the prior permission of the publisher.

Printed in Spain 10-98/2

MICHELIN TYRE PLC
Tourism Department
The Edward Hyde Building
38 Clarendon Road
WATFORD Herts WD1 1SX - UK
☎ (01923) 415000

MICHELIN TRAVEL PUBLICATIONS
Editorial Department
One Parkway South
GREENVILLE, SC 29615
☎ 1-800 423-0485

CONTENTS

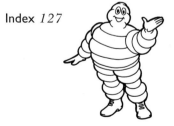

INTRODUCTION

The Loire Valley lies at the heart of France and serves as the nation's dividing line between north and south, marking its changes in weather and its tastes in wines, meats and cheeses. In the course of the river's journey from the mountains to the ocean, the valley bends westwards at the Sancerre vineyards, where it is at its most green and pleasant, then flows along the royal route of châteaux from Chambord to Angers.

It is for these châteaux that the valley is most celebrated – over 300 are listed in the Touraine region alone, but at least a score or more await the more ambitious sightseer. These palaces and fortresses have witnessed some of the most romantic and turbulent moments in French history. Today, they stand serene, elegant, formidable, grandiose – their stories often enchantingly presented in *son et lumière* (sound and light) shows. But the Loire offers much more besides these fairytale castles. Along the way, according to your taste, there are some fine Romanesque and Gothic churches and monasteries, while away from the architectural monuments there is rich fishing for pike (perch and trout in the river itself, carp and perch in the ponds of Sologne), canoeing and other watersports for the energetic, bird-watching for the more contemplative, street theatre in the larger cities, horse-shows at Saumur, the great 24-hour motor race at Le Mans and wine-tasting at picturesque towns such as Sancerre, Vouvray and Chinon.

The châteaux of the Loire are renowned the world over for their serene elegance. Château du Moulin, near Lassay-sur-Croisne, was built by Philippe du Moulin in the 15C.

4

GEOGRAPHY

The Loire river extends for 1 020km (637 miles), travelling north from its source in the Cevennes to begin a broad westward arc in Burgundy that takes it to the Atlantic at Nantes. Flanked by the forests of Sologne to the south and vast wheat fields of the Beauce to the north, the river swings south-west at Orléans into the best known part of the wide fertile valley that has gained the nickname '**The garden of France**'. In the region of Orléans and Blois, the river banks are lined with poplars and weeping willows, market gardens, fruit orchards and the exquisitely planned formal gardens and forests surrounding the châteaux.

The Loire's tributaries and neighbouring

The river Loire flows in wide, meandering bends.

rivers offer magnificent settings for many of the **royal residences**: Chenonceau straddles the waters of the Cher; Chinon stands on a hillside above the Vienne; Loches towers above the Indre, which the château at Azay-le-Rideau uses as a natural moat; while Ussé's castle finds its defences on a cliff above the river. Through a serene countryside of gently rolling hills, the Loir river (without an 'e') flows parallel to the main valley, past Châteaudun's castle perched on a promontory, before dividing the town of Vendôme into a few islands.

Ideal wine-growing soils of pebble and granitic sands, over a chalky bedrock, have given the region three groups of distinguished **vineyards**. South-east of Orléans, Sancerre is renowned for its white wines but equally appreciated by connoisseurs for its estimable reds and rosés. Touraine boasts the fine whites of Vouvray and Montlouis, and the reds of Chinon and Bourgeuil. The neighbouring Anjou country shares with Touraine a claim to the light, fruity Saumurs, along with the coveted dry white Savennières, and popular light rosés for the summer.

The local creamy yellow tufa, soft and porous as an undersoil but hardening into 'travertine' when exposed to the air, provides the Loire with a perfect rock from which to carve out its subterranean wine-cellars – ideal for developing champagne-style sparkling whites. The same rock, at the coveted **quarries** of Bourré, outside of Montrichard, has produced particularly handsome white stone for the construction of the châteaux. In the cliffs above the river, or in underground quarries, storage houses, workshops and whole

These troglodyte dwellings in the wine-growing area around Saumur are still inhabited.

villages of **troglodyte dwellings** can be found. Some, like those near Saumur and around Doué-la-Fontaine, are still inhabited. The tufa caves and quarries have also created ideal conditions for cultivating mushrooms in **champignonnières** (mushroom-beds).

Besides the **market gardens**' highly esteemed asparagus, and salad vegetables, the Loire is reputed for its fruit, especially pears, Anjou cultivating the famous Williams to rival the valley's delicious Beurré Hardy and Passe-Crassane. The greengage (in French *Reine-Claude*) was named after François I's Queen Claude while she was living at Chambord.

The **rose gardens** around Orléans and Doué-la-Fontaine have achieved international fame, as have the tulips, lilies and gladioli of Blois.

For those looking for a wilder landscape, there are the forest, heaths and marshes of the **Sologne** and the **Forest of Orléans**. To the south, in the Berry region, is the **Parc Naturel Régional de la Brenne** (Brenne Regional Park), with its many lakes. Deer and wild boar still roam some of these places. The smaller oak and beech forest of **Bercé**, north of the Loir, is also popular with walkers.

HISTORY

As far as recorded history is concerned, the Loire Valley is first mentioned in 52 and 51 BC when the **Carnutes**, a Gallic tribe, fiercely attacked the invading Roman forces of **Julius Caesar** around Orléans and Saumur. Despite brutal repression, however, it was not until Emperor Augustus's reign that the region was pacified and annexed to

Roman Gaul. The valley supplied the empire with much appreciated wheat, wine and Angers pottery. Gallic settlements at Angers, Tours and Orléans were Romanized with a forum, public baths, theatres and government buildings. By the end of the 2C AD, renewed unrest made it necessary to add ramparts to these settlements.

Invaders and Feudal Barons

In the 4C, **Christianization** began with the preachings of St Maurille at Angers and St Martin, the pioneering Bishop of Tours. With the Roman Empire on the decline, the valley was invaded first by the **Vandals**, and then the **Huns** who besieged Orléans in 451; the town held out until reinforcements arrived.

Over the next 500 years, first **Visigoths**, then **Franks** and **Normans** fought for

This effigy of Eleanor of Aquitaine marks her resting place in Fontevraud Abbey.

control of the rich Loire country. The invasion of **Arabs** from Spain was repelled by Charles Martel between Poitiers and Tours in 732. Subsequent Carolingian rule, under Charlemagne and his successors, was in turn challenged by murderous, plundering Normans who advanced upriver as far as the monastery of St Benoît and were halted only by a treaty in 911, creating the duchy of Normandy.

The turmoil left the region in the hands of feudal barons, each with his own army and currency, and castles sprang up on every strategic highpoint in the valley. By the 10C, the king of France had his château in Orléans, while the region's other major forces were the counts of Blois, controlling Tours, and their arch-rivals, the counts of Anjou. One of the latter, **Henri Plantagenêt** (Henry Plantagenet), married **Eleanor of Aquitaine** and became King Henry II of England, with territories stretching from Normandy down to the Pyrenees. He lived mainly in the château at Angers.

English control of the region was halted in 1202 when Philippe-Auguste seized all the provinces held by King John, thereafter known to the French as Jean sans Terre (John Lackland). Most of the valley was entrusted to the dukes of Anjou, but the **Hundred Years' War** brought the English back in the 14C, devastating the Loire farmland and leaving the population decimated by fierce battles, famine and plague. From his refuge in the Château de Chinon, the future Charles VII accepted **Joan of Arc**'s offer 'to boot the English out of France'. Invoking divine inspiration, she led a revitalized army and lifted the siege of Orléans in 1429, an event which, despite her

A statue of Louis XII adorns the main portal of Blois Château.

execution two years later, heralded the end of English rule.

Renaissance Glory and Wars of Religion

In the late 15C and throughout the 16C, the mild climate and great hunting forests made Touraine popular with **Charles VIII**, **Louis XII** and **François I**. The royal residences at Amboise, Blois and Chambord prompted their wealthy financiers to emulate them with equally splendid châteaux at Chenonceau and Azay-le-Rideau. This outpouring of Renaissance talent in the Loire Valley also found expression in the school of poets known as **La Pléiade** (*see* p.17) and celebrated painters such as Jean Fouquet (born in Tours), Jean and François Clouet and even Leonardo da Vinci, who spent his last years at Amboise (*see* p.19).

However, this period of creative harmony did not last. Responding to the spread of the Reformist ideas of Martin Luther and John Calvin (who studied law in Orléans and Bourges from 1528 to 1533), the Catholic Church began burning Protestant **Huguenots** at the stake. Galvinized by the executions, the Protestant movement spread and the Loire Valley became a violent focus of the **Wars of Religion**. At Amboise, in 1560, a group of Huguenot aristocrats seeking freedom of worship from François II – and retribution against the Guises, their Catholic arch-enemies – were arrested, hanged or beheaded. Huguenots reacted with a wave of vengeful plunder, causing bloody Catholic reprisals, notably at Angers. The **St Bartholomew Day Massacre** of Protestants, launched from Paris in 1572, left over 1 000 dead in Orléans alone.

To extract himself from the overwhelming power of the Catholic League in 1588, **Henri III** organized the assassination of its leader, **Henri Duc de Guise**, in the Château de Blois, and was in turn assassinated the following year. With him went the Valois dynasty that had so favoured the Loire Valley. It took his Bourbon successor, **Henri IV**, a further ten years to restore peace to the region.

Quiet Times Before the Revolution

The strong centralized monarchy, ushered in by the cardinals **Richelieu** and **Mazarin** and consolidated by Louis XIV, reduced the Loire Valley – perhaps not ungratefully after all the centuries of turmoil – to a quiet backwater. 'Exiled' to Blois, **Gaston d'Orléans**, brother of Louis XIII, instigated an occasional plot to assassinate Richelieu or to oust Mazarin, but these attempts at conspiracy were quickly foiled and before long the prince settled down peacefully to rebuild his château.

The Catholic Church bolstered its position by expanding the monasteries and building new seminaries for a better-educated clergy. Of the old Protestant bastions, only the great Saumur Academy survived. That, too, succumbed to Louis XIV's **Revocation of the Edict of Nantes** in 1685, ending Protestant freedom of worship and driving the valley's Huguenots into exile in Switzerland, Germany and England.

Nonetheless, political and religious peace permitted slow but steady economic growth. Market gardens and the wine trade expanded, while textiles prospered until the 18C, with silk manufacture at Tours thriving for a while, against stiff competition from Lyon. A new system of canals increased the

This statue of Cardinal Richelieu, by Ramey, stands in the park which once contained his château, at Richelieu.

valley's river traffic. As the main port, Orléans moved industrial goods and agricultural produce from all over the country, while supplying the nation with sugar from the town's own refineries.

Opinion along the Loire towards the **French Revolution** of 1789 divided largely between town and country. In urban centres the bourgeoisie and workers responded enthusiastically to the new ideas, with the merchants, in particular, profiting from the resale of confiscated church and royal property, whereas the peasants, particularly in the Anjou region, resented a new tax system no less oppressive than that under the Ancien Régime. The religious reforms also upset the more pious rural parishes more than the towns. Consequently, in 1793, the counter-revolutionary royalist army of the Vendée region to the south found widespread support among rebellious Loire Valley peasants in seizing Cholet, Saumur and Angers. Barely six months later, the Revolutionary troops recaptured the towns, leaving thousands dead.

Wars and Peace
The region took a back seat in France's wars in modern times. During the **Franco-Prussian War** of 1870–71, it was to Tours that the ardent French republican **Léon Gambetta** made his spectacular flight in a hot-air balloon from besieged Paris to lead the Resistance against the German forces. In 1917, Tours was chosen as the headquarters for the **United States Army**'s effort in the **First World War** and consequently American troops were garrisoned all along the Loire.

In October 1940, **Marshal Pétain** met **Adolf Hitler** at Montoire, west of Vendôme, to negotiate France's position vis à vis Nazi Germany. Soon after, the **Gestapo** began its interrogation and torture of Resistance fighters in the Loire region. The **Demarcation Line** between occupied France and the *'zone libre'* under the Vichy government passed along the Cher river, between Tours and Loches. The Loire Valley was liberated by American troops and French Resistance fighters in August and September 1944.

Peacetime in the second half of the 20C has seen the rapid development of the region as one of France's most popular tourist destinations. In 1952, François I's Chambord was the first of the Loire châteaux to stage a *Son et Lumière* show. The whole region's economy was boosted by the inauguration in 1989 of the high-speed TGV express train service linking Paris, through the Loire, to the Atlantic.

PEOPLE AND CULTURE

As befits a region that traces the cultural dividing line between north and south, its inhabitants are known for their moderation and calm temperament. Foreign visitors will find the people of the Loire, in town and country alike, reassuringly easy-going and straightforward.

Appropriately, too, in the historic home of so many kings of France, the French spoken here is still regarded as being the purest in accent. As Dante in Tuscany had given Italian its first literary form with his *Divine Comedy*, so it was at Orléans that the French language achieved its first literary recognition with the 13C *Roman de la Rose*, a 22 000-line poetic allegory of love composed by **Guillaume de Loris** and **Jean de Meung**.

Rabelais' memory is preserved in this small museum in his home town, La Devinière.

The Loire Valley was the birthplace or chosen home for many renowned writers. **François Rabelais** (1494–1553), doctor, monk and comic genius, grew up in Chinon and went to school in Angers. At banquets washed down with plenty of good red Chinon wine, local gourmands like to toast the legendary appetites of Rabelais' heroes, Gargantua and Pantagruel. With more dignified elegance, the 16C school of poets known as **La Pléiade** was formed by seven Loire Valley poets. They were led by **Pierre de Ronsard** (1524–85), from the Vendôme area, esteemed for the courtly grace of his sonnets, and scholarly **Joachim du Bellay** (1522–60) who, besides a lyrical tribute to his Anjou village of Liré, wrote a spirited defence of French as a literary language.

In the same patriotic tradition, philosopher **René Descartes** (1596–1650), born in the Touraine, chose to publish his great *Discours de la Méthode* (1637) in French rather than the Latin then favoured for philosophical writings. His famous dictum, 'I think, therefore I am,' known both in its French and Latin form – 'Je pense donc je suis (Cogito ergo sum)' – might be regarded as merely the most exquisite expression of the commonsense that distinguishes the people of the Loire Valley.

In the 19C, **Alfred de Vigny** (1797–1863), cool aristocratic Romantic poet and novelist, portrayed his native Touraine in the historical novel, *Cinq-Mars*.

But the region found a more lusty champion in **Honoré de Balzac** (1799–1850), many of whose novels of *La Comédie Humaine* depict in intricate detail his beloved Loire Valley. Born in Tours, he frequently fled from his troubles in Paris to the Château de Saché (near Azay-le-Rideau), where a wealthy friend gave him a room in which he wrote *Le Père Goriot* and *Le Lys dans la Vallée* (Lily in the Valley). The latter takes place in the countryside surrounding the château.

Orléans-born poet and progressive Catholic polemicist **Charles Péguy** (1873–1914) is revered in the region for his great poem dedicated to Joan of Arc, and among intellectuals for his impassioned defence of Captain Dreyfus.

At the northern limit of the Loire Valley region, in the broad, flat Beauce country,

Marcel Proust (1877–1922) remembered his childhood days spent in the village of Illiers, immortalized in his novels as Combray.

Quite apart from the great architecture of its châteaux and churches (*see* p.20), the region also had its share of illustrious painters. **Jean Fouquet** (1420–80) was born in Tours and gained recognition with his portraits and landscapes, many of them depicting the Loire, as the finest French painter of the 15C. Flemish artist **Jean Clouet** (1485–1541) worked in Tours for Louis XII and François I, who appreciated his distinguished portraits. He was succeeded by his son **François Clouet** (c 1515–72), born in Tours. François served as court painter to four French kings, expanding his scope beyond portraiture to more sensual subjects of classical mythology.

But the greatest of all the artists to grace the banks of the Loire river was **Leonardo da Vinci** (1452–1519). In 1516, the ageing master was invited by François I to live at Amboise in the Clos-Lucé manor near the château (*see* pp.45-46). Leonardo brought in his baggage three paintings for his host, all now hanging in the Louvre: the *Mona Lisa*, the *Virgin and Child with St Anne* and *John the Baptist*. All that remains of the last years of work of this quintessential Renaissance man are some plans for canalizing the Loire to Romorantin and drying out the Sologne marshes, in addition to architectural drawings that inspired parts of Chambord's château and perhaps Blois. He is also said to have organized the Amboise court's festivities. François I later told sculptor Benvenuto Cellini that one of his greatest joys was his almost daily conversations with Leonardo about philosophy and the arts.

Architecture of the Loire's Châteaux and Churches

Châteaux

Over the centuries, the resources of the royal treasury and wealthy bishoprics have endowed the Loire Valley with a brilliant array of secular and religious monuments. The region's earliest castles, such as **Loches** and **Chinon**, made use of hilltop Gallo-Roman fortresses (*castrum*). Made mostly of wood, they were erected on embankments topped by wooden palisades with a central watchtower.

By the 10C, when the valley's barons were able to share the royal prerogative of castle-building, the tower developed into a four-square castle keep enclosing an inner courtyard. Over the next 300 years, stone masonry replaced wood as the castles incorporated residential palaces built up on steep earthen mounds or, as at **Blois** and **Langeais**, at the edge of a promontory. The keep's banquet hall, apartments, kitchens and chapels were protected behind massive stone ramparts with towers and turrets. Changing warfare techniques and the greater weaponry expertise acquired in the Crusades led to a circular rather than a square castle keep. Deep, dry moats separated the outer walls, which bristled with yet more towers boasting sophisticated new battlements.

After the Hundred Years' War, the château-builders gradually turned away from military defences and put greater emphasis on the amenities needed for a royal or noble residence: larger windows, ornate state-rooms, libraries, music rooms and even bathrooms. If the towers did retain their battlements, they were now, as at **Sully**, embellished by cone-shaped 'pepper-pot' roofs.

The golden years of the 16C Renaissance ushered in an atmosphere of elegant opulence and gaiety: stately staircases, Italian-style galleries with coffered ceilings, vast ballrooms and throne-rooms. The moats at **Chenonceau**, **Azay-le-Rideau** and **Chambord** no longer served to repel enemies, but instead merely reflected the beauties of watchtowers and castle keeps. The effect was completed with landscaped and formal gardens, nowhere more in evidence than at **Villandry**.

Churches

The region's churches also present important landmarks in French architecture. East of Orléans, the Byzantine-influenced Carolingian church at **Germigny-des-Prés** dates back to the 9C. Nearby, **St-Benoît-sur-Loire** possesses one of the finest Romanesque basilicas in the country. At the other end of the valley, the 12C abbey-church of **Fontevraud** presents the ambulatory and radiating chapels characteristic of Romanesque in the Anjou. **Angers** itself made its mark in the transitional Gothic style with its 12C cathedral built with one broad nave and no aisles. The so-called 'Angevin vaulting' – multiple-ribbed swelling vaults mounted on slender columns – are a fine feature of the 13C **Église St-Serge** (Church of St Serge).

The Flamboyant Gothic style, with its flame-like stone tracery on the windows, is well represented in St Gatien at **Tours**, La Trinité at **Vendôme** and the Sainte-Chapelle in **Châteaudun**.

Detail of the roof at Chambord, with its elaborate adornments.

EXPLORING THE LOIRE VALLEY

MUST SEE
Newcomers to the Loire Valley are sometimes overwhelmed by the scores of châteaux and other attractions the region has to offer. Arranged here alphabetically are ten suggestions of places to include on a first visit.

Angers★★★
Steeped in history, with splendid Gothic churches and a formidable fortress containing magnificent tapestries, this is also an excellent place to taste the region's wines and fine cuisine.

Château d'Azay-le-Rideau★★★
Set in tranquil country, the town stands on the Indre river. Its château, surrounded on three sides by water and lush greenery, is a jewel of Renaissance architecture.

Map of the Loire Valley.

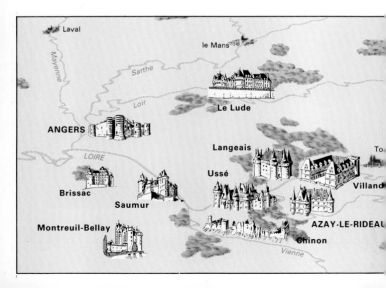

Blois★★
Towering over the delightful old town and sandwiched between the cathedral and the river, Blois' hilltop château exemplifies four centuries of architectural styles.

Château de Chambord★★★
Biggest of the Loire châteaux and built in brilliant white stone, Chambord has a famous dual staircase to the turrets and chimneys on the roof terrace, plus a grand view of the hunting forest.

Château de Chenonceau★★★
The château's construction of arches spanning the Cher river makes this the most enchanting of the Loire Valley's Renaissance palaces. It was home to Henri II's mistress, the great beauty Diane de Poitiers.

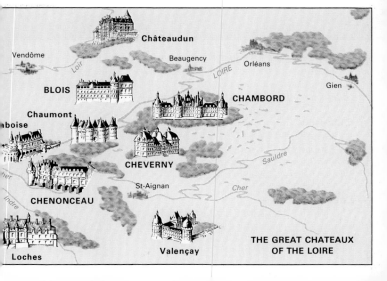

THE GREAT CHATEAUX OF THE LOIRE

Château de Cheverny★★★

Family home of Hurault de Cheverny, this cool, white château built in 16C Italian style retains a comfortable, lived-in atmosphere.

Chinon★★

A charming old town, with wine-cellars and a wine museum. The remains of the château bear witness to the story of Joan of Arc's meeting with Charles VII.

Loches★★

This medieval hill-town nestles against its imposing feudal castle, which was both a

Catherine de' Medici was responsible for the lovely formal gardens at Château de Chenonceau.

royal residence and a notorious prison.
There are beautiful views of the Indre river.

Tours★★

A friendly town with a fine Gothic cathedral,
medieval streets around Place Plumereau, a
good museum containing works by
Mantegna, Rembrandt and Delacroix, and a
summer music festival.

Villandry – Château and Gardens★★★

This late-Renaissance château is renowned
for its elegant Spanish-style interiors and its
exquisite gardens, landscaped on three
levels.

AROUND ORLÉANS

The eastern segment of the Loire Valley
covered by this section is set in a fertile
region of farmland and forest shared in
medieval times by the dukes of Orléans and
the counts of Blois. Today, both these towns
make good bases, each lying within easy
reach of the major sights.

Orléans★

This large but quiet town is an important
commercial centre for agricultural produce
and regional manufacturing. Despite the
onslaughts of the Wars of Religion, the
bombs of the Second World War and, not
least, some ruthless, modern urban
planning, enough monuments have survived
to give a fair idea of the illustrious role
played by Orléans in French history.

For the **Carnutes**, its strategic site at the
point where the Loire river turns west
towards the Atlantic made it ideal as the
centre of their pre-Roman Gaul. Julius
Caesar destroyed this rallying point of Gallic

resistance in 52 BC. His successors rebuilt it as Aurelianorum, which gave the city its present name. During the Hundred Years' War, the English siege of this vital strategic bridgehead on the Loire river was broken by **Joan of Arc**, earning her the title, 'Maid of Orléans'. The victory is still celebrated in the city with processions and fireworks every 7 and 8 May (*see* p.90).

The imposing **Cathédrale Ste-Croix★** (Cathedral of the Holy Cross) remains the city's principal monument and a centre for the cult of Joan of Arc. In the 300 years following its destruction in 1586 by Protestants during the Wars of Religion, what was originally a largely Romanesque pilgrimage church took on its present late Gothic appearance. The towers and imposing porch framing four great statues

The west front of Ste-Croix, in Orléans, is an impressive sight.

of the Evangelists Matthew, Mark, Luke and
John were completed just before the French
Revolution. Inside, notice the superbly
carved 18C wood-panelling in the choir.
Joan of Arc's story is told in 19C stained-
glass windows.

Near the cathedral, the **Musée des Beaux-
Arts**★★ (Fine Arts Museum) features
important French artists – Louis Le Nain,
Boucher, Watteau, Courbet, Gauguin and
Maillol – on the first floor. On the second
floor are paintings by Velázquez (*St Thomas*)
and Correggio (*Holy Family*), plus a
Tintoretto portrait and works by Van Dyck
and Ruysdael.

Across the Place de l'Etape, the 16C red-
brick **Hôtel Groslot** is the city's noble Town
Hall and one-time residence of kings visiting
Orléans.

To the west is the city's main square, **Place
du Martroi**, popular for its lively cafés and
restaurants surrounding a statue of Joan of
Arc (1855). The 'martyrs' of the square's
name are a reference to its location over an
early Christian cemetery.

The tall gabled **Maison de Jeanne d'Arc**★
(House of Joan of Arc), where she stayed in
1429, has been lovingly rebuilt in its original
form on an otherwise thoroughly modern
square named after a more recent French
saviour, General de Gaulle. Costumes,
model weaponry and audio-visual shows
illustrate the events of the momentous siege
of Orléans.

Housed in a handsome Renaissance
mansion known as the **Hôtel Cabu**, the
Musée historique★ (Historical Museum)
traces the region's history dating back to
Gallo-Roman times. The exhibits include
ancient bronzes, medieval sculptures,

Joan of Arc, Maid of Orléans, who saved the city in 1429 and whose victory is celebrated every year.

tapestries, ceramics and other local craftwork.

From the tourist information office (Place-Albert Ier), get a map of the signposted walking-tour around the most attractive examples of Orléans' medieval and Renaissance houses. These are illuminated at night. Some of the best are on **Rue Royale** and **Rue de Bourgogne**.

Église de Germigny-des-Prés★
(Germigny-des-Prés Church)

The church at Germigny-des-Prés, east of Orléans, is one of only a handful of Europe's churches surviving from the Carolingian era. It was originally the chapel for the home of **Bishop Theodulf**. At the end of the 8C, Charlemagne gave the Orléans diocese to Theodulf, an erudite cleric from northern Spain; Germigny was part of the bishop's country estate. Surviving from that original chapel, built to a Byzantine-style, Greek Cross plan, is the eastern apse, which is adorned with a fine **mosaic★★** depicting the hand of God flanked by two archangels beneath two cherubim. Notice, too, the translucent **alabaster windows** in the central lantern which lights the altar.

St-Benoît-sur-Loire★★

Just east of Germigny-des-Prés, the **Basilique St-Benoît★★** (Basilica of St Benedict) is one of the true treasures of French Romanesque architecture. The site's sacred origins date back to the annual assemblies held here by the Druids at the time of the Gallic Carnutes. Begun in 1067, the basilica was erected at the Benedictine abbey to house the hundreds of pilgrims visiting the remains of St Benedict which were brought

Carved pillars support the porch and bell-tower of the Basilica of St Benedict, at St-Benoît-sur-Loire.

here from the abbey of Monte Cassino in Italy at the end of the 7C.

The remarkable **porch**** is surmounted by a bell tower, with richly carved capitals on the pillars supporting its arches. Although the lofty **nave**, completed in 1218, points the way to a Gothic architectural transition, the earlier **chancel**** is resolutely Romanesque in style, with its ambulatory for solemn processions and multiple chapels for overflowing crowds of worshippers. The huge **crypt*** protects the earthly remains of the founder of Western monasticism, which are kept in a modern reliquary.

In the village **cemetery** is the tomb of

eminent French poet and painter **Max Jacob**, who sought refuge in St-Benoît during the Second World War; he was arrested by the Gestapo and died in captivity.

Château de Chambord★★★

West of Orléans is Château de Chambord, the biggest and among the best known of the Loire Valley châteaux, and a pioneer in the art of *son et lumière* shows. Beginning as little more than a hunting-lodge for the counts of Blois, the château was transformed under its royal owner, François I, into the most sumptuous of Renaissance palaces.

The stupendous **park** is a remnant of the great forest where the king came to hunt deer and wild boar, but still covers some

The Cosson river was diverted in order to fill the moat of the elaborate Château de Chambord.

5 500 ha (over 13 500 acres) and is well worth a separate visit. The west side is open to visitors and from four observation-decks wild boar can be seen at feeding time, in the early morning or at sunset. Stags can be heard bellowing at nightfall during the mating season. Tours are available in horse-drawn coaches. Its moat is a diversion of the Cosson river, a tributary of the Loire; if funds had allowed, François I would have diverted the Loire itself.

To build Chambord, François I emptied the royal treasury – and that of several churches. Begun in 1519, the exterior was finished by 1537 but the royal residence was not completed until 1545, just two years before his death.

As a precursor to Versailles, Chambord was much appreciated by Louis XIV, who visited it for performances of new plays by Molière. Although the first night of *Le Bourgeois Gentilhomme* did not raise so much as a smile from the Sun King, he nevertheless came back for a second look, congratulated the author, and its success was assured.

Though the brilliant white château's elegant appearance does not bear the slightest hint of a military fortress, the design is a clever Renaissance variation on the feudal theme of a central four-square castle keep, with a tower at each corner. Some scholars like to attribute it to the architectural doodles of Leonardo da Vinci, working down the road at Amboise. Approached through the **Cour d'honneur** (ceremonial courtyard), the keep is flanked by a chapel on the left and royal apartments on the right. The French Revolution did away with most of the furnishings, but Louis

XIV's **royal chamber**, on the first floor of the castle keep, boasts some handsome wood-panelling installed in the 18C.

At the centre of the keep is the famous **double staircase.** Two concentric spirals wind around each other to the roof in such a way that two people mounting and descending might do so without meeting – vitally important in carrying on extramarital affairs, a major Renaissance pastime.

Before culminating in one single spiral, the staircase takes you to Chambord's crowning glory, the **roof-terrace**. This presents an astonishing maze of ornate chimneys, cupolas, turrets, lanterns and other staircases. It was also a grandiose viewing platform for parades and the departure and return of the royal hunt.

The ingenious double staircase at the Château de Chambord has, over the centuries, provided much amusement for children and aided many a secret tryst.

Château de Cheverny★★★

This family-owned castle has an elegance that is at first glance more austere than many of its fellow châteaux along the Loire. This derives in large part from the formal unity of the design carried out by Count Hurault de Cheverny from 1604 to 1634. It has a symmetrical style of Italian inspiration, a neat geometry of curving domes and quadrangular slate roofs flanking the triangular roof above the narrow, central core.

In contrast, the interior is quite intimate. The count's descendants still dwell in part of the château, which occupies land that has been in the family for over 700 years. For once, the Renaissance and 17C furnishings are original to the château. They include outstanding Flemish tapestries in the **Salle à manger** (dining room), along with mural paintings by Jean Mosnier illustrating the

The armoury, the largest room in the Château de Cheverny, contains 15C and 16C arms and armour, and a tapestry from the Gobelins.

adventures of Don Quixote. The finest decoration is to be seen in the **Chambre du Roi** (Royal Chamber), with a grand 16C canopied bed, Gobelins tapestries and a sculpted fireplace beneath the splendid coffered ceiling. A Titian portrait of Cosimo de' Medici graces the **Grand Salon** on the ground floor. The largest room in the château is the **Salle d'armes** (armoury), containing arms and armour from the 15C and 16C.

Hunting enthusiasts can visit the **kennels** to see the family's 70 foxhounds and a **trophy room** boasting 2 000 sets of deer antlers. A new attraction is an enormous hot-air balloon, holding up to 30 people, which is moored to the ground and rises up to

Detail of the ornate staircase at Cheverny.

150m (450ft), providing superb views of the surrounding countryside.

You will catch glimpses of the great hunting forest of **Sologne**, most of it off-limits to the public, on drives between Chambord and Cheverny.

Blois★★

With its impressive location forming an amphitheatre on slopes overlooking the Loire, the city invites the idle stroller – as much as the ardent château-visitor – to explore its tangle of medieval streets. The architecture of the extensive château covers four centuries of the town's chequered history, from the 13C after the counts of Blois had ceded their fiefdom to the king of France, through the royal grandeur of the

Renaissance to the murderous days of the Wars of Religion and the conspiratorial but quieter times of Gaston d'Orléans in the 17C.

To the right of the façade of the **château★★★**, overlooking the Place du Château, is part of the feudal castle. Distinguished by its pointed roof, it houses the 13C assembly hall of the Etats généraux (feudal parliament). The main building is a stately brick and stone wing built by Louis XII (1498), who is depicted in an equestrian statue over the main porch. This is a 19C copy, but the bawdy stone carvings on a couple of the window-supports to the left of the porch are originals.

Cross the inner courtyard to the **terrace** for a view of the Loire and the last vestige of the feudal ramparts, the **Tour du Foix** (Foix Tower). Back in the courtyard is the Gothic

The sturdy bridge links the attractive old quarter of Blois to the left bank of the Loire.

choir of the **Chapelle St-Calais**, Louis XII's
private chapel. Opposite, dominating the
Aile François Ier (the François I wing), is the
elegant **Grand escalier** (staircase) set in an
octagonal cage which provided a series of
balconies from which courtiers watched the
château's ceremonies. On the first floor is
the room of the notorious Catherine de'
Medici; here the scheming mother of three
French kings kept her secret papers,
jewellery and, say conspiracy-buffs, a
collection of poisons, stored in wall
cupboards opened by a concealed foot-
pedal. The second floor was the scene of the
château's most famous crime, the murder of
the Duc de Guise, by which Henri III rid
himself of the overbearing leader of the
Catholic party in the Wars of Religion. The
guide will show you the rooms where the

*François I's
elaborate external
staircase at Blois
Château enabled
courtiers to view
events in the
courtyard below.*

duke was done to death with 23 stab wounds delivered by eight knifemen and 12 swordsmen. Closing off the courtyard is the more sober classical 17C wing built for Gaston d'Orléans, **Aile Gaston-d'Orléans**.

On the square across from the château, the **Maison de la Magie-Robert-Houdin** is scheduled to open, presenting the mysterious and fascinating realm of magic. The museum is named after the 19C 'father of modern conjuring', Robert-Houdin of Blois, watchmaker, and the first magician to use elements of electricity.

Of the town's churches, the Gothic-Romanesque **Église St-Nicolas★** (Church of St Nicholas) is the most attractive, once part of a Benedictine abbey. **Cathédrale St-Louis** (St Louis Cathedral) was rebuilt in the neo-Gothic style after its destruction by a

The spires of the Church of St Nicholas overlook Blois' historic centre.

hurricane in the 17C. It is a good place from which to begin a walk through the town's delightful old streets, in particular the **Rue du Puits-Châtel** and the **Rue des Papegaults**. At the top of a grand stairway linking the upper town and the lower town on the river bank, the **Denis Papin statue** is one of the town's more curious landmarks. It is dedicated to a man regarded as the 17C inventor of steam-powered machinery and the pressure-cooker.

The imposing Château of Chaumont-sur-Loire was once home to Catherine de' Medici.

Château de Chaumont-sur-Loire★★

Just 16km (10 miles) south-west of Blois, this late Gothic and early Renaissance château was the home of Catherine de' Medici. The

queen mother maliciously forced her rival, Diane de Poitiers, to accept it in exchange for the grander palace of Chenonceau (*see* p.46). It remains a fine monument in its own right, with **Catherine's Chambers** being a principal feature, beautifully decorated with appropriate 17C furnishings. The **gardens** are a special attraction, scene of an annual international garden-landscaping competition in the summer.

AROUND TOURS

The Touraine is the heart of the Loire Valley, boasting the most charming and popular châteaux, well-preserved medieval towns and prestigious vineyards. Its history produced an exciting mixture of high romance, torture, massacre and murder most foul.

Its central location, good restaurants and hotels make the city of Tours the perfect base for anyone wanting to stay in just one place while touring the whole valley.

Tours★★

Spread out between the Loire and Cher rivers, this bright and airy town is a haven of civilized living. Despite wartime bombing in the centre and some hasty modern reconstruction, it has preserved attractive historic neighbourhoods, affording pleasant, leisurely walks.

During the 4C, when St Martin, a converted soldier, made Tours the focus of his mission against paganism, the Gallo-Roman citadel of the Turons became a cradle of French Christianity. The relics of the town's first bishop drew pilgrims from all over Europe – his renown has resulted in over 4 000 churches bearing his name throughout France, and many more beyond. The city's ecclesiastical activity also duly attracted eminent intellectuals: 6C historian Grégoire de Tours and, at the end of the 8C, Abbot Alcuin, Charlemagne's English court scholar who brought wider literacy to Tours by opening its first major schools. The tradition continues to this day with, in addition to a university of over 25 000 students, important centres for urban archaeology, Renaissance studies and the teaching of French to foreign students from all over the world.

Extensive restoration work and new college faculty buildings down by the Loire have breathed new life into the historic quarter around **Place Plumereau★** where charming 15C half-timbered and stone houses surround cheerful outdoor cafés. From here, a covered passage leads to the little garden square of **Place St-Pierre-le-Puellier**, part of which was once a Renaissance cloister. **Rue Briçonnet★** is itself

Place Plumereau, in Tours, has some wonderful half-timbered houses.

almost a museum of Tours' architectural styles – simple Romanesque, stately Gothic, a Renaissance mansion with wooden statues and a fine classical façade of the 18C. On the **Rue du Grand-Marché**, gabled houses of red brick and silvery slate line the bustling pedestrian zone of shops, bars and cafés, with craftshops on the nearby **Quartier du Petit Saint-Martin**.

Of the 11C Romanesque **Ancienne Basilique St-Martin** (Old Basilica of St Martin), almost all that remains are the **Tour Charlemagne** (Charlemagne Tower), south of Rue Châteauneuf, and **Tour de l'Horloge**

The Charlemagne Tower is one of only two remnants of the once enormous Old Basilica of St Martin. The building to the right is the New Basilica.

(Clocktower) across the Rue des Halles. The great pilgrimage church was smashed by Protestants in 1562 during the Wars of Religion, and crumbled into ruin after the French Revolution. The saint's remains are entombed in the crypt of the **Nouvelle Basilique St-Martin** (New Basilica of St Martin), built here in neo-Byzantine style in 1924 and still the object of a pilgrimage on the saint's day, 11 November.

Nearby, in part of the old cloister on Rue Rapin, the **Musée St-Martin** (St Martin's Museum) documents the saint's life and exhibits marble sculptures dating back to the first basilica of 470, and mosaics and murals from the Romanesque church.

On the west side of the city's historic centre, the 15C Flamboyant Gothic façade of **Cathédrale St-Gatien★★** (St Gatien Cathedral) gives way to a more sober Gothic interior, largely completed a century earlier and enhanced by the exquisite **stained-glass**

St Gatien Cathedral, Tours, has some lovely stained-glass windows, such as this rose window.

The towers of St Gatien Cathedral exemplify Gothic architecture at its most extravagant.

windows★★ in the transepts and choir. The choir is a masterpiece of restrained elegance. Built onto the church's north wall is the peaceful **Psalette**★ (cathedral cloisters), so named for the psalms sung there by the cathedral's canons.

Immediately to the south, the town's **Musée des Beaux-Arts**★★ (Fine Arts Museum) is housed in the archbishop's palace (17C and 18C). Its most important works are two paintings by Mantegna, part of a Verona altarpiece, works by Rubens and Rembrandt and French 18C paintings by Boucher, Nattier and Rigaud.

The lovely river promenade on **Quai d'Orléans** gives you a view of the scanty remains of the town's once formidable **château**. Of the largely 13C fortress, the chief feature is the **Tour de Guise**, a pepperpot-roofed tower named after the young Duc de Guise imprisoned there after his father was assassinated (*see* p.13). With the 18C **Pavillon de Mars**, it houses the exhibition rooms of the **Historial de Touraine**, a museum illustrating the history of the Touraine region with many waxworks figures. They present, with considerable fantasy, scenes such as royal weddings, Protestant Huguenots preparing to flee the country and the momentous 1920 Congress of Tours which launched the French Communist Party.

Amboise★★

For a good first view of the château and town (east of Tours), stop on the **bridge** linking the little island of St-Jean to the left bank of the Loire.

Amboise enjoyed its moment of glory in the 16C as the home of two Renaissance princes – one a royal patron of the arts, François I, the other 'merely' an artist, the king's guest, Leonardo da Vinci, who died there in 1519 (*see* p.19).

With most of it demolished in the Napoleonic era, the **château★★** has retained a largely Gothic appearance in the 15C **Logis du Roi** (royal apartments) built by Charles VIII. It was here, in 1560, that dozens of Protestant aristocrats and their soldiers were arrested and hanged from an

iron balcony, one by one, as they arrived at the castle to present a petition to the king. The adjacent **Tour des Minimes or des Cavaliers** is famous for its large ramp used by horsemen to climb to upper terraces of the château. At the top, you can enjoy a good **view**★★ of the Loire Valley – and the iron balcony. Away from the river, the **Chapelle St-Hubert** (Chapel of St Hubert, 1491) is an admirable example of Flamboyant Gothic, particularly in the sculpture over the entrance. It is believed that Leonardo da Vinci was buried here.

Leonardo's last home, the charming red-brick and white stone **Le Clos-Lucé**★, is a short walk south-east of the château. His

The impressive château at Amboise dominates the surrounding town.

One of Leonardo da Vinci's mechanical creations, displayed in the basement of his home, Clos-Lucé.

host, François I, is said to have reached Clos-Lucé from the château via the secret underground passage. The rooms of the manor are decorated with authentic Renaissance furnishings and the kitchen is notable for its monumental fireplace. The basement is devoted to a fascinating exhibition of some 40 models of Leonardo da Vinci's machines *(see* p.19).

Château de Chenonceau★★★
South of Amboise, this most enchanting of châteaux extends on arches to form a bridge across the Cher river, the tranquil waters reflecting the consummate beauty of its pure Renaissance design. The fairytale river-

setting amid formal gardens and green forests attracts many visitors to Chenonceau (the name of the adjoining village is spelt with an added 'x') and is the most popular of all the Loire châteaux – visitors are fast approaching one million a year. A self-guided tour with brochure from the ticket-office enables you to go at your own speed and avoid 'traffic jams'.

The building of this charming château and its grounds was overseen by three women. On land bought in 1513 by royal financier Thomas Bohier, his wife, daughter of the mayor of Tours, built the main body of the castle, the rectangular **logis**, with its

The serene beauty of Chenonceau, reflected in the river Cher, stands as a tribute to the women who shaped its development.

The long gallery at Chenonceau was used as a hospital during the First World War, and marked the boundary with occupied France in the Second World War.

neat arrangement of towers and turrets at each corner. Diane de Poitiers, beautiful mistress of Henri II, introduced the first formal **gardens** and added a bridge to reach the south bank of the river. Later, her archenemy and Henri's widow, Catherine de' Medici, seized it, laid out the **park** and erected the elegant two-storey **gallery** on the bridge to give the château its final distinctive form. (In the Second World War, Resistance fighters used the 60m/197ft gallery as an escape route, as it straddled the Demarcation Line separating the German Occupation zone from the rest of France.)

On the ground floor of the logis some impressive Flemish tapestries can be seen in the **guard room**, and there is a marble bas-relief of the Virgin and Child in the adjoining **chapel**. Notice the ornate stone hearth in **Diane de Poitiers' bedroom**. Her portrait by Primaticcio hangs in **François I's bedroom**. Other works in the gallery include paintings by Rubens, Nattier and Rigaud.

Loches★★

Further south, this fortified town presents a captivating contrast between its idyllic setting overlooking the Indre river and the forbidding medieval citadel. Its strategic hilltop position has made it a prime military bastion since Gallo-Roman times. In the Middle Ages, England's Henry II strengthened its fortifications and Richard the Lionheart and France's Philippe-Auguste vied for its control. In the 15C, Louis XI imprisoned and tortured his enemies here in foul cells and iron cages. The château was also a love-nest for Charles VII and his beloved Agnès Sorel. Earlier, in 1429, Joan of Arc came to Loches and convinced Charles VII to travel on to Reims to be crowned.

The sturdy walls of the château at Loches hold secrets of a sordid past.

The **château★★** and **donjon★★** (castle keep) are built separately at the north and south ends of the ramparts. Entrance is through the massive 11C **Porte Royale★** (Royal Gate), with twin towers added 200 years later.

Rue Lansyer leads to **Église St-Ours★** (Church of St Ours) with a fine Romanesque porch and two distinctive octagonal pyramids rising between the towers to form domes over the crossing between the nave and transepts.

The château looms north of the church with the 13C **Tour Agnès-Sorel** (Agnès Sorel Tower) at its right-hand corner. In the royal apartments, the lady's legendary voluptuous beauty can be seen in a portrait by Jean Fouquet (original in Antwerp) showing her as a bare-breasted Virgin Mary. Her more demure marble **funerary monument★** stands nearby. A portrait of her beloved king can be seen in the **chamber of Charles VII**. It was in the nearby state room, with its monumental fireplace, that Joan of Arc urged Charles to become king after her victory in Orléans.

The overwhelming mass of the castle keep offers a more sinister aspect of Loches. Its infamous cages, made of wood and iron, were destroyed by peasants in the French Revolution, but it continued to serve as a gruesome prison at least until 1926 and probably again in the purge of French collaborators in 1945. After visiting the prison-cells and torture chambers in the **Tour Ronde** (Round Tower) and **Martelet** dungeon, you might like to climb the main keep's staircase of 157 steps to a terrace with a peaceful view of the town and mellow landscape of the Indre Valley.

It was in this room in the château at Loches that Joan of Arc persuaded Charles VII to accept the crown.

From the Martelet dungeon, walk along the **medieval ramparts★** for a good view of the citadel and town. Take time to stroll around the old town's winding, narrow lanes. Points of interest are the 15C crenellated town-gate, **Porte des Cordeliers★**, **Tour St-Antoine** (St Anthony's Tower) and the imposing Renaissance **Hôtel de Ville★** (Town Hall) adjoining the **Porte Picois** town-gate.

Gardens★★★ and Château★★ deVillandry

Going west from Tours, the late Renaissance **Château de Villandry★★**, one of the last to be built (1536) on the Loire, has design elements that reflect the taste of a court moving closer to Paris: square pavilions, rather than round towers, flanking the main building and an arcaded gallery around the courtyard. The château interior has been tastefully furnished by its most recent owners in 16C, 17C and 18C Spanish style.

Laid out on three different levels, the **gardens★★★** represent one of France's best examples of Renaissance landscaping, combining the geometric art of Italian gardeners brought in by Charles VIII and the French tradition of monastic gardens. The uppermost level is a **water-garden**, beneath it an **ornamental garden** of flower-beds illustrating allegories of love and music,

The gardens at Villandry, some of the most elaborate in France, were lovingly restored at the beginning of this century.

These beautiful geometric designs in the gardens at Villandry symbolise allegories of love.

and at the lowest level a fantastic **kitchen garden** of nine geometrically arranged vegetable-plots and beds of fruit-trees.

Château d' Azay-le-Rideau★★★

This gem among the valley's châteaux – for Balzac, a meticulously cut diamond – benefits, like Chenonceau, from a woman's touch. In this case, it was the wife of financier Gilles Berthelot who in 1518 conceived this lovely, ornate Renaissance re-interpretation of a traditional feudal fortification. The diverted waters of the Indre river serve not as a defensive moat but as a glorified reflector pool in which Azay can admire its pepperpot-domed silhouette. The sensually rounded corner turrets are for bedchambers and music rooms, not vantage points for firing arrows. Battlements adorn the château, they have become a pretty

The wife of the 16C financier Gilles Berthelot supervised the building of the charming Château of Azay-le-Rideau; but fortunes changed, and Berthelot was forced to flee, abandoning the château.

necklace and no guard ever made his rounds along the roof's purely decorative balustrade.

The interior is attractively decorated with Renaissance furnishings, Flemish tapestries and a 15C oak canopy-throne. One of the most impressive features is an elaborately decorated grand staircase.

In contrast to the delights of the château, is the memory of 350 soldiers who were massacred on the orders of the 15-year-old Charles VII while on a visit to the town in 1418. After being insulted by the Burgundian guard, he had the whole garrison executed and the village burned to the ground.

Chinon★★

This balmy, amiable town stretches out along the Vienne river, its medieval houses nestling against a long ridge topped by the remains of the castle and its ramparts. Palm trees carry a hint of the south and, in the childhood home of François Rabelais, Chinon's bracing wines – fragrant reds and dry rosés – are there for the drinking in cellars and wine-bars throughout the town.

Chinon lies at the heart of an important wine-growing region.

England's Henry II saw Chinon as a useful vantage point from which to oversee his French dominions and he died there in 1189. King John was unable to hold on to it against Philippe-Auguste and it was still in French hands when Joan of Arc had her

Parts of the Château de Chinon still stand proudly on the Vienne river, despite attempts to destroy it following the French Revolution.

historic first meeting here with Charles VII in March of 1429. To test her vaunted divine powers and see whether she could recognize him, Charles dressed up as a courtier and hid among 300 others in the great hall of the palace. She picked him out immediately and told him the English would be defeated and he would be crowned king of France. Despite this, she still had to undergo three weeks of interrogation by doctors and scholars to ascertain that she was not a witch. In April, she was given arms and an army to set about liberating Orléans – and France.

The sprawling **château★★** was progressively dismantled after the French Revolution, but parts of the **Château du Milieu** (Middle Castle), have survived. Entrance is through the tall 14C **Tour de l'Horloge**, a clocktower with a bell still tolling the hours and an exhibit illustrating the life of Joan of Arc. In the **Logis Royaux** (royal apartments), the first-floor grand hall in which Joan recognized Charles VII has disappeared except for its great fireplace. A 17C Aubusson tapestry depicts the historic event.

The main thoroughfare of **Old Chinon★★**, lined with medieval half-timbered houses, is **Rue Voltaire** which continues under its old name of **Rue Haute St-Maurice** as it passes below the castle walls. The **Musée animé du Vin et de la Tonnellerie** (Museum of Wine and Barrel-Making) is housed in a wine cellar, where full-scale animated models demonstrate the wine-making process.

The Tour de l'Horloge, in Chinon, rings out the hour.

Carved from the hillside stone are the **Caves Painctes** (Painted Cellars), made famous by Rabelais's accounts of Pantagruel's carousing *(see* p.17); although they have lost their frescoes, meetings of a Rabelaisian fraternity continue to be held here.

The neighbourhood's most attractive houses are grouped around the **Grand Carroi★★**, their gabled redbrick, wood and stone façades dating back to the 14C and 15C.

The **Musée du Vieux Chinon et de la Batellerie** (Museum of Old Chinon and River-boats) is housed in a medieval assembly hall in which Richard the Lionheart is believed to have died in 1199. Local folk art and model boats are well displayed, along with a Delacroix portrait of Rabelais.

TOURAINE VINEYARDS

In the wine-producing towns, tourist offices and wine-co-operatives belonging to the

Vines growing near Chinon.

A wine cellar, cut into the hillside at Vouvray.

Maisons du Vin provide details of tours and tastings in the region's vineyards.

Vouvray

On the Loire's right bank, east of Tours, the vineyards producing some of the country's most reputable white wines, still and sparkling, are grouped around the village of Vouvray which has preserved many of its old **troglodyte dwellings**. These are hewn, like the wine cellars, from the region's white chalky stone. The **Espace de la Vigne et du Vin** (Grape and Winemaking Centre) tells the story of winemaking from Roman times to the present day, with a tasting at the end of the visit.

Bourgueil

Set on the slopes north of the Loire, the many vineyards of Bourgueil are open to visitors wishing to taste or buy their fine, light red wines. These can also be tasted at the rock-hewn **Cave touristique de la Dive Bouteille** (Cellar of the 'Divine' Bottle), which presents an impressive collection of old wine-presses.

The town's **Église paroissiale** (Parish Church) has a monumental Gothic choir beyond the more simple Romanesque nave. Opposite are the handsome stone-arched **Halles** (Covered Market), forming the rear of the old Town Hall.

AROUND ANGERS

There is an ineffable tranquillity to the gentle greenery of the Anjou region and the lazy flow of the Loire, with its flat meadows bordered by pretty hedgerows. Here the

Prosperous old Angers sits peacefully on the river.

châteaux are less spectacular and there are more orchards, market gardens and vineyards.

Angers★★★
Stronghold of feudal barons and medieval English kings, the town is built on both banks of the Maine river, just 8km (5 miles) north of the point at which it flows into the Loire.

Angers prospers today from its commerce in wines, the region's farm produce and flowers, and a growing electronics industry. Yet it also remains the region's major centre for tapestries, both ancient and modern.

The **château**★★★ was built in the early 13C

Parts of the sumptuous Apocalypse Tapestry have remained in remarkably good condition, considering its mistreatment over the years.

by Louis IX, 'Saint Louis' to the French, the massive ramparts with their 17 round towers presenting the perfect image of the feudal fortress. Standing 50m (164 feet) high, they were originally even taller, with pepperpot domes on the towers, until their demolition was ordered in the 16C by Henri III – but interrupted at his death. From the tallest tower, **Tour du Moulin** (Mill Tower), on the north corner, you get a good **view★** of the château, the gardens laid out in the dry moat and the town beyond. On the east side of the ramparts is a **medieval garden** planted

with roses, daisies, lavender and vines in a
style favoured by Anjou's Good King René.

Begin your visit of the château's interior
with the dukes' spacious and elegant 15C
late-Gothic **chapel**. Notice in the ceiling the
Anjou Cross which became the Cross of
Lorraine, and was adopted by General de
Gaulle in his combat against the German
Occupation. A spiral staircase leads to the
logis royal (royal apartments) which boast a
magnificent collection of 15C and 16C
tapestries, notably four richly coloured
panels of the *Tenture de la Passion* (Passion
Tapestry).

Housed in a specially built modern gallery
is the most famous of Angers' tapestries, the
monumental 14C **Tenture de l'Apocalypse★★**
(Apocalypse Tapestry). It was woven,
probably in Paris, for Duke Louis I of Anjou
to adorn weddings and other ceremonial
occasions. Originally 130m (426 feet) long
and 5m (16 feet) high, it consisted of six
huge panels each showing an eminent
person seated before a series of pictures
illustrating the New Testament Apocalypse
of St John. Miraculously preserved after
centuries of abuse as stable-cloths, carpeting
and covers for orange-trees in winter, 76
scenes have survived to portray the trials and
triumphs of Jesus and the Church – with an
occasional touch of levity such as a rabbit
frolicking along the tapestry's lower border.

East of the château is the largely 12C
Cathédrale St-Maurice★★ (Cathedral of St
Maurice), with a third central tower added
in the 16C. (St Maurice is revered by Angers
citizens, as a converted Gallo-Roman soldier
who lived in the 4C, he was cruelly executed
for refusing to kill his fellow Christians.)
Above the door of the porch is a

The elaborate carved figures decorating the House of Adam, Angers, were symbols of the wealth of the 16C merchant for whom it was built.

handsomely sculpted enthroned Jesus surrounded by the symbols of the four Evangelists.

The interior presents an impressive example of Anjou Gothic – lofty ribbed vaults forming domes over an exceptionally wide nave without aisles. This effect is further refined in the domed vaults over the transept and choir. Besides the many **Aubusson tapestries** adorning the walls, the cathedral's treasure is its **stained-glass windows**★★ dating from the 12C to the present day. Binoculars are needed to appreciate the detail of Jesus's Passion and

Glory in the transept rose windows (15C) and the saints' lives in the choir (13C), notably Peter on the left, Martin and Thomas of Canterbury on the right.

Among the town's many attractive old houses, pride of place must go to the 16C **Maison d'Adam★** (House of Adam), behind the cathedral, with its richly sculpted wooden posts and beams. The **Logis Barrault** is a late-15C residence built by the mayor of Angers, now housing the **Musée des Beaux-Arts** (Fine Arts Museum). Its collections include Romanesque and Gothic sculpture and paintings by Watteau, Fragonard, Boucher and Corot, and drawings by Géricault and Delacroix. Another mayor built the Renaissance **Hôtel Pincé★**, now the **Musée Turpin-de-Crissé**, presenting Egyptian, Greek and Etruscan antiquities and a remarkable collection of Chinese and Japanese art.

The **Galerie David d'Angers** on Rue Toussaint, housed in a restored 13C abbey church, features a fascinating collection by the town's most celebrated sculptor, Pierre-Jean David (1789–1856). Displayed are studio casts of scores of historical figures, among them Gutenberg and Goethe, Napoleon Bonaparte, Victor Hugo and Balzac.

The **Église St-Serge★** (Church of St Serge) has a 13C **chancel★★** with an exquisite example of Anjou Gothic, a dozen delicately ribbed vaults on slender columns, known as **Angevin vaulting**, which provide a stark contrast to the robust pillars of the nave, built 200 years later. Notice the delicate grey-toned stained-glass windows, portraying Old Testament prophets, on the north wall and the Apostles on the south.

On the right bank of the river, tapestry-buffs might like to visit the **Musée Jean-Lurçat et de la Tapisserie contemporaine★★** (Museum of Contemporary Tapestry) installed in the medieval Ancien Hôpital St-Jean (Hospital of St John). The museum presents tapestry in its contemporary form as revived by Jean Lurçat (1892–1966). His master-work, 80m (262 feet) long, is the *Chant du Monde* (*Song of the World*, 1957) series, his exalted modern response to the *Tenture de l'Apocalypse* (*see* p.62) which he had discovered 19 years earlier. Nearby is the **Centre Régional d'Art Textile** (Regional Textile Art Centre), providing studios for artists to display, explain and sell their modern tapestries.

Église de Cunault★★ (Church of Cunault) Standing on the left bank of the Loire, east of Angers, the superb Romanesque **abbey church** of Cunault was built by Benedictine monks in the 11C. Its sturdy bell-tower topped by a 15C spire dominates a façade unadorned except for its blind arches and the solidly sculpted Enthroned Virgin surrounded by angels above the porch.

The interior has an exhilarating spaciousness catering to vast throngs of pilgrims and solemn processions of the Benedictine order, hence the wide ambulatory and radiating chapels around the choir. In the otherwise austere décor, an astounding collection of 223 meticulously sculpted capitals stand out. Apart from a pair at the entrance to the choir – to the right, a group of nine monks, to the left, St Philibert receiving a sinner – you will need binoculars to appreciate the detail of the impressive Romanesque craftsmanship.

Saumur★★

This proud town is known for its horses, its wines, and its toy factories and manufacture of carnival masks. The cavalry tradition, which dates back to the royal horsemen of the 18C, has continued with training of the tank and armoured corps of the modern age. Parades and performances of the **Cadre Noir** (Black Squad), as the cavalry élite is known, are an annual attraction.

The best views of Saumur are to be found from the watchtower of the château.

In the 16C, Saumur was declared by Henri III as a safe haven for Protestants during the Wars of Religion. Henri IV appointed as its governor Philippe Duplessis-Mornay, a great

Saumur at night.

soldier and theologian known to the Catholics as 'Pope of the Huguenots'. The Protestant Academy he founded was closed after Louis XIV revoked the Edict of Nantes, which guaranteed freedom of worship, in 1685. After their church was demolished, most of the town's Huguenots emigrated.

Rising above a platform of star-shaped ramparts built by Duplessis-Mornay in the 16C, the severe exterior and more decorative inner courtyard of the **château** reveal the mainly 14C building as both palace and fortress. It was in turn a prison and barracks before housing its present-day museums: the **Musée d'Arts décoratifs★★** (Decorative Arts Museum), devoted to medieval and Renaissance wooden and alabaster sculpture, tapestries, furniture and paintings, and porcelain of the 17C and 18C; the **Musée du Cheval★** (Horse

Museum), tracing the history of the horse and equestrianism across the world, with a fascinating collection of saddles, stirrups and spurs; and the **Musée de la Figurine-Jouet** (Toy Museum), a delightful collection of ancient and modern toy soldiers and models of the kings of France.

At the heart of the town's old quarter north of the château, the **Église St-Pierre** (Church of St Peter) is a Gothic edifice with a fine Romanesque doorway and good 16C **tapestries★** in its nave. Around the church in the narrow streets winding down to the river are the best of the old houses, notable for their half-timbered gables or wrought-iron balconies.

The **Hôtel de Ville★** (Town Hall) derives its fortress-like appearance from being incorporated in the city wall when it originally bordered the Loire river.

This monument in Saumur is a memorial to cavalrymen who trained at the military school here.

A leisurely way to explore Saumur.

South-west of the château, the **Église Notre-Dame-de-Nantilly★** (Church Notre-Dame-de-Nantilly) is an admirable Romanesque building. It has 18 intricately sculpted capitals in the nave and some remarkable 15C, 16C and 17C tapestries.

France's military history since the 18C is well presented at the **Musée de l'École de cavalerie★** (Cavalry School Museum), just west of the city centre. The nearby **Musée des Blindés★** (Tank Museum) presents tanks from a dozen countries, including the German Panzer, the British Churchill and the American Sherman.

Fontevraud-l'Abbaye★★
(Fontevraud Abbey)

After 150 years as one of France's cruellest prisons, this abbey on Anjou's eastern border with Touraine has been recently restored as a cultural centre to recall something of the astonishingly innovative Fontevriste order, founded in 1101.

Robert d'Arbrissel (1045–1117) created the abbey with a motley collection of aristocratic ladies and reformed prostitutes, clerics and vagabonds, invalids and lepers. They had five separate monasteries, each with its own church, the whole governed, after the founder's departure, by an abbess. From 1115 to 1789, Fontevraud had 36 abbesses, half of them of royal blood. Notable among them were Jeanne-Baptiste, daughter of Henri IV, and Gabrielle de Rochechouart de Mortmart, sister of Louis XV's mistress, Madame de Montespan, and known as the 'queen of abbesses'.

After the order was abolished during the French Revolution, Napoleon turned the abbey into a notorious prison that closed in 1963.

Tour guides explain the fascinating history of Fontevraud Abbey.

The gisant of Richard the Lionheart lies in Fontevraud Abbey.

Since the demolition of several tiers of prison-cells, the great 12C **Église abbatiale★★** (abbey church) has recovered the spaciousness of the Gothic nave, the cupolas rising from finely sculpted capitals. **The tombs of the Plantagenets★★** – reclining mortuary statues of England's Henry II, his wife Eleanor of Aquitaine (who was a nun at Fontevraud) and their son Richard the Lionheart – have also been restored.

On the south side of the church is the imposing Renaissance **Cloître Ste-Marie** (cloister) of the aristocratic nuns. Adjoining the cloister's eastern gallery, in the **Salle capitulaire★★** (chapter house), is a series of 16C paintings of the abbesses. Running along the southern gallery is the imposing Romanesque **refectory**, its Gothic ceiling added after a fire.

The Mary Magdalene Convent, for reformed prostitutes, was built in the north-east corner of the abbey.

Apart from the abbey church itself, the most striking of the monastery buildings is the monumental **kitchen★★**, the only Romanesque kitchen to have survived in France. Its nest of conical chimney domes, topped by the octagon 27m (88 feet) above the ground, corresponds to the interior's cooking-hearths. The kitchen was used not only for cooking but for smoking meats and fish.

The chimneys of the huge kitchen at Fontevraud.

EXCURSIONS

With such a wealth of sights to see in the
Loire Valley itself, we have limited
excursions to just two: south, from **Sancerre**
through the **Sologne** region to **Valençay**; and
north, from **Châteaudun** via **Vendôme** to **Le
Mans**.

Sancerre to Valençay

Sancerre★, in the far east of the region, is a
charming little Berry town perched on a
rocky spur above its vineyards, reputed for
their white wines – but try the delicate reds
and rosés, too. Explore the old quarters
around La Nouvelle-Place and the Rue des
Pressoirs.

*Vineyards spread
out like a
patchwork quilt
below the town of
Sancerre.*

   On the border of Berry and Sologne,
Aubigny-sur-Nère★ was a stronghold of the
Stuarts, Scottish allies of Charles VII and
other French kings against the English.

Romorantin-Lanthenay, childhood home of François I, has some lovely 16C timber-framed houses.

Their 16C **château** is now the Town Hall and a summer festival still celebrates the 'Scottish connection'.

Romorantin-Lanthenay★, to the south-west, is the ancient capital of the Sologne hunting region, with the **Musée de Sologne★** (Sologne Museum) devoted to the fauna and flora of the nearby forest. Among the many enchanting gabled and half-timbered houses, the old **Hôtel St-Pol** is renowned as the scene of a mock battle between François I and the townsmen, which cost the king his hair.

Valençay has a handsome **château★★**, bought by Talleyrand, the great diplomat-survivor, in 1803. Sample the goat cheese, whose distinctive truncated pyramid shape is said to have originated when Napoleon lopped the top off with his sword at Talleyrand's table.

Château de Valençay was built c1540 by Jacques d'Estampes to display his new-found wealth – the result of marrying a rich wife.

Châteaudun to Le Mans

Châteaudun★★, at the northern end of the peaceful Loir valley (without an 'e'), was the last home of Dunois, the 'Bastard of Orléans', whose military prowess helped Joan of Arc to victory. The **château★★** stands

The beautifully carved choir stalls complement the soaring Gothic nave of Trinity Abbey, Vendôme.

on a promontory high above the river. It has the appearance of a Gothic fortress on the exterior, and an ornate palace in its inner courtyards. Its 15C **Sainte-Chapelle** (Chapel) has a noteworthy group of polychrome **statues★★**.

Following the river south, **Vendôme** is built across islets formed by several arms of the Loir river. After a look at the Flamboyant Gothic **Abbaye de la Trinité★** (Trinity Abbey)

Châteaudun has a rather austere exterior.

with its superbly carved choir stalls and nearby a **museum**★ with mural paintings and religious art, take a boat trip around the islands.

Continuing eastwards, **Lavardin**★ has an almost excessively romantic castle ruin up on a rocky promontory. The Romanesque **Prieuré St-Genest** (Priory of St Genest) was a popular stopover in the Middle Ages for pilgrims on their way to St James's shrine at Santiago de Compostela in Spain. Inside the **Mairie** (Town Hall), take a look at two halls dating from the 11C.

North of the Loir is the pretty **Forêt de Bercé** (Bercé Forest), ideal for a stroll or picnic among the stands of oak, beech and chestnut.

Le Mans**, north on the Sarthe, is, of course, renowned above all for its 24-hour car race in June (motorcycles in April or May). The circuits are usually open to the public on non-race days. The **Musée de l'Automobile de la Sarthe**** (Motor Museum) is located near the Bugatti Circuit.

Those more interested in historic monuments should not miss the **Cathédrale St-Julien**** (St Julian's Cathedral), a 12C Gothic cathedral with magnificent flying buttresses on its **chancel**** and a fine sculpted **porch**** on the south side. Gallo-Roman **ramparts*** enclose the medieval town, and there are elegant houses on the **Grande-Rue** and **Rue Reine-Bérangère**.

The famous racetrack at Le Mans is the setting for many exciting races.

GAZETTEER

Beaugency★ – 29km (18 miles) south-west of Orléans
A medieval town on the Loire's left bank, which for many centuries was an important crossing point. It has a Romanesque abbey church, **Église Notre-Dame★** (Church of Notre-Dame), and a château housing the **Musée Régional de l'Orléanais★**, the region's folklore museum.

Château de Beauregard★ – 6km (4 miles) south of Blois
A Renaissance château near Cheverny famous for its 363 historic portraits in the **Galerie des Illustres★★** (Portrait Gallery).

Béhuard★ – 18km (11 miles) south-west of Angers
This quaint 15C village stands on an island in the Loire river, the houses surrounding the **Église Notre-Dame** (Church of Notre-Dame), which is built on a rocky outcrop.

Blancafort★ – 9km (5.5 miles) north-east of Aubigny-sur-Nére
The 15C red-brick château has 17C pavilions, a handsome library and a dining room. There is an interesting church with a clocktower-porch in the

The Portrait Gallery at Beauregard is a parade of 14C-17C celebrities.

The reception room at the Château de Brissac.

pretty village. Nearby, off the
D 8 to Concressault, is the
Musée de la Sorcellerie
(Witchcraft Museum) with
displays on witchcraft, goblins
and dragons.

Château de Boumois★ – 7km
(4 miles) north-west of Saumur
This charming 16C château
has a medieval appearance.
A portrait of England's Queen
Elizabeth I hangs in the hall.

La Bourgonnière★ – 9km
(6 miles) south-east of Ancenis
The elaborately fortified 16C
Chapelle St-Sauveur★ (Chapel
of Our Saviour) here features a
remarkable altarpiece.

Château de Brissac★★ – 20km

(13 miles) south-east of Angers
Set in a splendid park of cedar
trees, this lofty Renaissance
château has first-rate tapestries,
elaborate ceilings and 18C
furniture.

Candes-St-Martin★ – 11km
(7 miles) south-east of Saumur
The village of Candes stands at
the confluence of the Loire
and the Vienne. The Gothic
church★ marks the spot where
St Martin of Tours died in 397.

Champigny-sur-Veude★ – 6km
(4 miles) north of Richelieu
Champigny has some fine 16C
houses and the Renaissance
stained-glass windows★★ in the
Sainte-Chapelle★ (Chapel) are

Interior of Sainte-Chapelle, Champigny.

among the region's best.

Champtoceaux★ – 10km (6 miles) west of Ancenis
Perched on a spur high above the west end of the Loire Valley, the village has a spectacular view of the river islands from the **Promenade de Champalud★**, behind the church.

Cléry-St-André★ – 15km (9 miles) south-west of Orléans
The 15C **Basilique de Notre-Dame★** (Basilica of Notre-Dame) is the burial place of Louis XI. The richly decorated Gothic pilgrimage **Chapelle St-Jacques★** (St James's Chapel) is off the south aisle.

Corniche Angevine★ – about 5km (3 miles) long
This winding road on the left bank of the Loire follows the cliff south of Angers, with lovely views of riverside villages and vineyards.

Doué-la-Fontaine★ – 19km (12 miles) south-west of Saumur
This village, built on a plateau, has numerous caves, used variously in the past as dwellings, wine-cellars, storehouses and stables. Other attractions are its excellent **zoo★★** and **Musée des commerces anciens**, a museum of traditional trades.

Château de Fougères-sur-Bièvre★ – 8km (5 miles) north-west of Contres
A feudal fortress with a beautifully timbered interior.

Gien★ – 60km (38 miles) east of Orléans
A first-rate hunting museum, **Musée International de la Chasse★★** (Hunting Museum), is installed in the château at the edge of Orléans forest and the Sologne. Gien is known for its *faïence* (glazed earthenware) and the factory, where both expensive hand-made items and modern mass-produced

services are made, is open to the public.

Grange de Meslay★ – 10km (6 miles) north-east of Tours
This remarkable 13C gabled tithe barn, with 15C timbering, is used for music festivals and art exhibitions.

Illiers-Combray – 40km (25 miles) north of Châteaudun
This market town, on the upper reaches of the Loir, is strictly for Marcel Proust fans. He spent his summers in Illiers and portrayed it as Combray in his novel *Remembrance of Things Past*. **Maison de tante Léonie** belonged to Proust's uncle and the museum evokes the writer's life and works.

Langeais★ – 23km (14 miles) south-west of Tours
The 15C **castle★★** has its original drawbridge, battlements and keep (10C). The apartments have been accurately furnished to portray life in the 15C and early Renaissance. Look out for the many fine tapestries, mostly Flemish. The Château de Planchoury (4km/2.5 miles from Langeais) houses the **Musée Cadillac** (Cadillac Museum), with a large collection of vintage cadillacs.

Lorris★ – 45km (28 miles) east of Orléans
Of interest in this small town is the Romanesque-Gothic **Église**

Notre-Dame★ (Church of Notre-Dame) and the **Musée Départemental de la Résistance et de la Déportation** (World War II Resistance and Deportation Museum), housed in a former railway station.

Le Lude – 50km (31 miles) north-west of Tours
The village overlooks the Loir. Outstanding **son et lumière,** shows take place at the 15C

The well-preserved battlements of the castle at Langeais.

Château du Lude★★. The Renaissance **Maison des Architectes** (Castle Architects' House) can be seen near the entrance.

Marnay – 6km (4 miles) west of Azay-le-Rideau
The eccentric **Musée Maurice Dufresne★**, a museum housed in a former papermill, is devoted to machines of all kinds, including the first draught-beer machine and army vehicles recycled as farm machinery.

Vallée de la Mayenne★ (Mayenne Valley)
The valley passes through unspoilt country north of Angers, offering river cruising and bird-watching. **Haras national de l'Isle-Briand★**, the national stud farm at L'Isle-Briand (22km/14 miles north

Grez-Neuville, at the heart of the Mayenne Valley.

of Angers), offers tours of the stables and riding school.

Meung-sur-Loire★ – 14km (9 miles) west of Orléans
A picturesque town with streams running alongside its narrow streets, a 13C **church★** and a château reflecting a variety of styles. It possesses an *oubliette*, an underground well where prisoners were put to die; the poet François Villon is supposed to be the only man ever to come out alive – he was

The kitchen at Meung-sur-Loire.

released by Louis XI.

Château de Montgeoffroy★ – 24km (15 miles) east of Angers
This beautiful château retains its original 18C furniture designed specially for the château, and paintings by Rigaud, Pourbus the Younger and Van Loo, among others.

Château de Montpoupon★ – 12km (8 miles) south of Montrichard
A Gothic Renaissance structure providing a rare insight into the day-to-day running of a château in the last century. The **Musée du Veneur** (Hunting Museum) displays

hunting costumes and
souvenirs.

Montrésor★ – 50km (31 miles)
south-east of Tours
Overlooking the Indrois, a
tributary of the Indre, this
enchanting old village nestles
beneath a **castle★** perched on a
rocky spur.

Montreuil-Bellay★ – 16km
(9 miles) south of Saumur
Prettily located on the Thouet
river, the town is dwarfed by its
huge **château★★**, which has an
impressive medieval kitchen
and vaulted wine-cellars, plus
fine 15C frescoes in the chapel.

Montrichard★ – 42km

(26 miles) south-east of Tours
Town on the Cher river with
cave dwellings, mushroom-
beds and cellars for the 'cham-
pagnization' of white wine.
Displays of **falconry** take place
during the summer at the
keep.

Pagode de Chanteloup★ –
3km (2 miles) south of Amboise
Situated at the edge of
Amboise forest, this French
version of a pagoda is all that
remains of the 18C château.
There are 149 steps up to the
top, where there is a fine view
of the Loire Valley.

The château of Montreuil-Bellay.

The ruins of the château at Montrichard perch above the town.

Pontlevoy – 5km (3 miles) north of Montrichard
The 18C buildings of the former **abbey★** include a refectory with a monumental Delft china stove and a 15C abbey church.

Manoir de la Possonnière★ – 1km (0.5 mile) south of Couture-sur-Loire
The 16C Renaissance **manor house★** of Possonnière belonged to Pierre de Ronsard, 'prince of poets'.

Richelieu★ – 62km (39 miles) south-west of Tours
This orderly, classical town was planned by Cardinal de Richelieu in 1631. Near the entrance to the park, which once contained the Cardinal's château, is a **statue of Richelieu** by Ramey. A **steam train** runs between Richelieu and Chinon, and there is a **railway museum** at Richelieu station.

Château du Rivau★ – 11km (7 miles) south of Richelieu
Nicely furnished Gothic-

The moated château of Sully-sur-Loire.

Renaissance **château**; it provided horses for Joan of Arc's soldiers en route to the siege of Orléans.

Saché – 6.5km (4 miles) east of Azay-le-Rideau

The room within the **château** where Balzac wrote *Le Père Goriot* and *Le Lys dans la Vallée* is kept intact. The village was home, as well, to the American sculptor Alexander Calder (1898–1976), whose work can be seen in the main square.

St-Aignan★ – 25km (16 miles) east of Chenonceau

The little town of St-Aignan, with its Gothic houses, 11-12C Romanesque **church★** and Renaissance **château**, stands on the Cher river in pretty woodlands. **Zoo Parc de Beauval★**, which includes a large tropical glasshouse, is 4km (2.5 miles) to the south.

Château de Serrant★★ – 2km (1 mile) north-east of St Georges-sur-Loire

An opulently furnished 16-18C château, with Flemish **tapestries** and a Renaissance staircase.

Chapelle de la Sorinière
(Sorinière Chapel) – 3.5km
(2 miles) east of Chemillé
A simple chapel, built in 1501,
with remarkable **wall-
paintings★** depicting the
Nativity and the Adoration of
the Magi.

Sully-sur-Loire★ – 41km
(26 miles) south-east of Orléans
The **château★** here is a moated
Gothic fortress, largely 14C,
with a beautifully preserved
medieval **timber★** roof in the
keep.

Château de Talcy★ – 40km
(25 miles) south-west of Orléans
Set amid Beauce farmland, this
battlemented fortress contains
fine tapestries, a 400-year-old
wine-press, and lovely inner
courtyards with a flower-
bedecked well and a dovecote.

Château d'Ussé★★ – 14km
(8 miles) north-east of Chinon
A 15C, multi-turreted white-
stone **château** in a rustic
setting with terraced gardens.
It is said to have provided
Perrault with the inspiration
for *Sleeping Beauty*. It contains
superb Flemish **tapestries** and
there is a fascinating salle de
jeux (games-room) with toy
trains and dolls' houses in the
castle keep. The elegant 16C
chapelle★ (chapel) is built in
Renaissance style.

The elegant Salle du Roi, in the Château d'Ussé.

WEATHER

The Loire Valley is blessed with a mild climate, without the extremes usually associated with the Continent. The renowned sweetness of the air and generally mellow weather have made it the epitome of *la douce France*, 'gentle France'. The valley is at its best in the spring, especially in May and early June, or during the golden days of autumn, till late October. The summers are mostly lazily warm, rarely unbearably hot, and the winters, although damper, particularly in the Anjou, are still frequently sunny.

CALENDAR OF EVENTS

The region's regular round of festivities covers cultural, sporting, religious, wine and other agricultural activities (check local tourist offices for exact dates). *Son et lumière* shows at the châteaux are generally limited to the summer months, June to September (*see* Entertainment p.102).

January/February: wine festivals at Angers, Azay-le-Rideau, Vouvray.

March/April: Fontevraud Abbey *Itinérances* music recitals (March–December); St Benoît-sur-Loire Easter vigil; Saumur international horse show jumping, Cadre Noir equestrian demonstrations from April to September; Bourgueil and Chinon wine festivals.

May: Le Mans motorcycle races; 7, 8 May Orléans feast of Joan of Arc, procession, fireworks; Saumur wine festival.

June: Chambord Game Fair, hunting and fishing; Le Mans 24-hour car race; Blois wine festival.

June/July: Classical music, choral and dance festivals; Sully-sur-Loire classical music, jazz and dance festival.

July: Orléans international jazz festival;
Anjou arts festival staged in châteaux in and
around Angers; Loches and Chinon musical
theatre festival; Blois street-theatre
(throughout summer); Doué-la-Fontaine
rose flower show; Saumur military tattoo.

August: (first weekend) Chinon Marché
médiéval (Medieval market), costumed
street-vendors, puppet-shows, dances,
craftwork, medieval cuisine; 15 August wine

The medieval market at Chinon is a colourful and lively event.

festivals at Vouvray and Amboise.
September: Fêtes Musicales de Touraine held at the Grange de Meslay.
October: international horse show at Le Lion d'Angers.
November: Montrichard wine festival.
24 December: St-Benoît-sur-Loire vigil and mass.

ACCOMMODATION

The Loire Valley boasts some of the most beautiful scenery in France. There are many excellent hotels and guest houses in the area, many offering spectacular views across the valley. Service Loisirs Accueil takes reservations for places to stay all over France. They are based in Paris at 280 Boulevard St-Germain, 75007 Paris, ☎ 01 44 11 10 44, but also have offices within most of the tourist offices in the Loire Valley area (*see* **Tourist Information Offices**), and an additional one (Loire) at 8 Rue d'Escures, 45000 Orléans, ☎ 02 38 62 04 88, Fax 02 38 77 04 12.

Logis et Auberge de France have numerous family-run hotels which generally provide comfortable accommodation with a friendly atmosphere and excellent regional cuisine. Their guidebook, containing 4 000 hotels throughout France, is available from tourist offices.

Self-catering is a good option in the Loire Valley, there are *gîtes* in abundance. These are usually with a regional flavour. For information contact Maison des Gîtes de France, 59 Rue St-Lazare, 75009 Paris, ☎ 01 49 70 75 75 or Maison de France, 178 Picadilly, London W1 ☎ 0891 244123.

Chambres d'hôtes provide bed and breakfast accommodation. Details of these

are available from Bed and Breakfast
(France), International Reservations Centre,
PO Box 66, Henley-on-Thames, Oxon,
RG9 1XS, ☎ (01491) 578803, Fax (01491)
410806; and also from the Gîtes de France
organisation. For information on youth
hostels, contact La Ligue Française pour les
Auberges de la Jeunesse, 38 Boulevard
Raspail, 75007 Paris, ☎ 01 45 48 69 84.

Recommendations

The *Michelin Red Guide France* lists a selection
of hotels, while the *Places To Stay Map* in the
Michelin Green Guide Châteaux of the Loire
indicates recommended places for overnight
stops. Here are a few recommendations:

Amboise
Le Choisel (*36 quai Ch. Guinot* ☎/fax 02 47
30 45 45) Very comfortable, charming hotel
with an excellent menu.

Angers
Anjou and restaurant Salamandre (*1 Bd Mar.
Foch* ☎ 02 41 88 24 82) Beautiful interiors.
Le Cavier (*8km/5 miles outside Angers,
La Croix-Cadeau* ☎ 02 41 42 30 45) The
dining room is housed in an old windmill.

Beaumont-en-Véron (5km/3 miles from
Chinon)
La Giraudière (☎ 02 47 58 40 36 fax 02 47
58 46 06) Small hotel, furnished in 16C
style.

Cangey (11km/7 miles east of Amboise)
Le Fleuray (*7km/4.5 miles north of Cangey on
the road to Dame-Marie* ☎ 02 47 56 09 25)
Lovely countryside house with restaurant.

Chênehutte-les-Tuffeaux
Le Prieuré (☎ 02 41 67 90 14) Secluded, set
in wooded grounds overlooking the Loire.

Chinon
Château de Marçay (*9km/5.5 miles from the*

D 116 ☎ 02 47 93 03 47 fax 02 47 93 45 33)
15C château, with park grounds, swimming
pool and tennis courts.

Fontevraud l'Abbaye
Hôtellerie Prieuré St-Lazare (☎ 41 51 73 16)
Set in the old priory of the Abbey.

Joué-les-Tours
Château de Beaulieu (*5km/3 miles south-west
Tours, 67 Rue Beaulieu* ☎ 02 47 53 20 26)
Very peaceful; meals served in the gardens.

Onzain (between Blois and Amboise)
Château des Tertres (*1.5km/1 mile along the
D 58* ☎ 02 54 20 83 88) Country house set in
parkland.

Saché (*6.5km/4 miles from Azay-le-Rideau*)
(☎ 02 47 26 88 77) 12C Inn. Rustic
atmosphere.

Sury-aux-Bois (40km/24 miles east of Orléans)
Domaine de Chicamour (*3.5km/2 miles south
of Sury-aux-Bois on the N 60* ☎ 02 38 55 85 42)
19C house set in a park.

FOOD AND DRINK

You can quite happily dine out in *le jardin de
France*, 'the Garden of France', eating or
drinking only local produce. The wines of its
vineyards, the freshwater fish, its meats,
game and poultry, its cheeses and the fruit
of its orchards make the Loire Valley
gastronomically self-sufficient. The cuisine is
like the climate, mellow and invigorating.

Hors d'Oeuvres

Also known as the *entrée*, which means
starter. The valley-grown asparagus (*asperges*)
are superb, served cold, luke-warm with a
vinaigrette sauce or mayonnaise, in an
omelette or even to dip in a couple of soft-
boiled eggs. For pâté, try the *rillettes*, a
speciality in Angers, Tours and Le Mans, of

Fresh produce on sale at the local market.

minced pork and perhaps duck blended with a light pork fat. This is sometimes a stuffing for hot *fouace*, a Loire version of pitta-bread. *Rillons* are pieces of pork breast cooked for hours and served cold.

Fish

Pike-perche (*sandre*), pike (*brochet*) and carp (*carpe*) are abundant in the Loire and its tributaries, served with a simple *beurre blanc*, light butter sauce with a little vinegar (speciality of Orléans) or white wine. A popular dish is *matelote d'anguilles*, eel sliced in a red wine sauce, preferably Chinon, with onions and mushrooms. Try, too, a plate of fried whitebait (*friture*).

Meat and Poultry

Pork is often cooked with prunes (*noisette de*

porc aux pruneaux), rabbit (*lapin* or *lapereau*) may be stuffed *à la solognote* with bacon and breadcrumbs. *Fricassée de poulet* combines the superb poultry of Le Mans with Loire Valley white wine for the cream sauce, adding mushrooms and onions. *Coq au vin* is also fine with a Bourgueil red for the sauce. Capon (*chapon du Mans*) is best skewer-broiled. If you want a simple steak, the beef from the Berry cattle south of the Loire is excellent, but rack of lamb (*carré d'agneau*) comes from outside the region. Game from Sologne may include partridge (*perdrix*), pheasant (*faisan*) or duck (*canard*).

Taking a break from shopping and sightseeing in one of the pavement cafés.

Vegetables
Besides the asparagus, try white mushrooms – a variety known as *champignons de Paris* but grown in great quantities around Saumur –

stuffed or cooked in cream, excellent green cabbage (*choux-verts*), and for salads, locally produced walnut oil (*huile de noix*).

Cheeses

Among the Loire's most appreciated goat cheeses is the little *Crottin de Chavignol*, produced near Sancerre and combining particularly well with its wines, often warmed and served on a lettuce leaf. The *Pyramide de Valençay* is more delicate. Another fine goat cheese comes from Sainte-Maure de Touraine; this distinctive cheese is stored in cylinders with a straw through the middle. *Olivet* is a cows' milk cheese from the Orléans area, sometimes blue or coated with the ash of vine-leaves. *Crêmet d'Anjou* is a heavenly concoction of white cheese with whites of eggs and whipped cream, served with sugar or strawberries.

Goat cheeses are a speciality in the Loire Valley.

Dessert

There is a cornucopia of fruit: strawberries from Saumur, apricots and pears from Angers, plums, greengages (*Reine-Claude*), and prunes from Tours. Most of them find their way into pies (*tourtes*), for which Tours is renowned, as is Orléans for its fruit preserves, and Angers for its wafer-thin pancakes (*crêpes angevines*), served with the town's orange liqueur, Cointreau, or with a compote of apples. The most famous dessert of all is the *Tarte Tatin*, the caramelized apple tart – which must be served hot – 'invented' by the Tatin sisters at Lamotte-Beuvron in Sologne.

Wines

Although searching out the red wines of the Loire Valley can be a rewarding experience (especially those of Chinon and Bourgueil), and Anjou produces wonderful rosé, it is really a region of delicious white wines. To the east are the flinty-dry Pouilly and Sancerre, immediately appealing and made

The wine-growing regions of the Loire Valley.

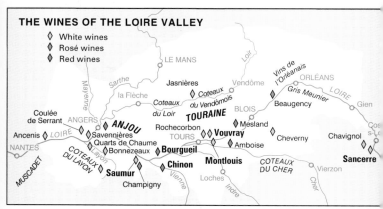

THE WINES OF THE LOIRE VALLEY

◇ White wines
◇ Rosé wines
◆ Red wines

from the Sauvignon grape. Downstream, before Tours, are the sweeter, more complex delights of Vouvray and Montlouis made from Chenin Blanc.

Like Touraine, the best wines of Anjou tend to sweetness. The sparkling wines from both Vouvray and Saumur are exciting and delicious.

Things get dry again in the Pays Nantais, to the west, where the grape best suited to seafood grows near the coast – Muscadet. Look for Muscadet '*sur lie*' to enjoy it at its best.

The region's most reputable liqueur is the orange-flavour Cointreau from Angers, which also produces other fruit liqueurs and *eaux de vie*.

Wine-tasting at the Maison du Vin in Saumur.

Recommendations

Unless you are a gourmand for whom sightseeing comes a distant second to eating, we recommend saving your main meal for the evening, most often back in the town where you are staying overnight. Only rarely will you find a restaurant near a great château with cuisine to match the latter's architecture. Here are a few suggestions (*see* also the Accommodation Recommendations p.93, which include some restaurants):

Blois

L'Orangerie du Château (*1 Av Dr J Laigret* ☎ 02 54 78 05 36) An elegant restaurant, with views of the château from the terrace.

Orléans

La Chancellerie (*Pl Martroi* ☎ 02 38 53 57 54) Moderately priced; in the town centre.

Tours vicinity

Rochecorbon: L'Oubliette (*6km/3.7 miles from Tours, Rte Parcey-Meslay* ☎ 02 47 52 50 49) Housed in a former troglodyte house.

Near Montbazon: Moulin Fleuri (*15km/9 miles from Tours* ☎ 02 47 26 01 12) Charming restaurant in an old windmill by the Indre.

Saumur

Les Délices du Château (*courtyard of the château;* ☎ 02 41 67 65 60) Delightful terrace overlooking the château gardens.

Les Menestrels (*11 Rue Raspail* ☎ 02 41 67 71 10) Rustic atmosphere, with exposed beams.

Fontevraud l'Abbaye

La Licorne (*Allée Ste-Catherine* ☎ 02 41 51 72 49) Set in a charming old house.

Le Mans

Le Grenier à Sel (*26 Pl Éperon* ☎ 02 43 23 26 30) A rustic house located in the old town.

Neuville-sur-Sarthe

Vieux Moulin (☎ 02 43 25 31 84) Old watermill on the banks of the Sarthe.

A potter at work in Poncé-sur-le-Loir.

SHOPPING

For many, the best of the Loire Valley's products to take home as souvenirs may be the **gourmet delicacies**. Wines are available from wine-cellars (*caves*) indicated by the wine-towns' Maison du Vin or tourist office. Good markets to shop at for gourmet foods – cheeses, pâtés, hams, fruit preserves – are Les Halles at Tours and Chinon's Sunday morning farmers' market on Place Général-de-Gaulle.

In Angers, **tapestry** as an art and as a decoration for the home has come back into vogue, revived thanks to the *Tenture de l'Apocalypse* masterpiece exhibited in its château (*see* p.62). Examples of the artists' work can be purchased in their studios at the **Centre Régional d'Art Textile** (Regional Textile Art Centre).

The valley's most spectacular market is Chinon's **Medieval market** in August (*see* p.91), when traditional crafts are on display – and for sale.

Tours stages a **flea market** (*brocante*) on Place de la Victoire every Wednesday and

ENJOYING YOUR VISIT

Saturday, and a market for regional
craftwork – wood-carving, silks and other
textiles, copper utensils and ornaments – on
Place de la Résistance every second and
fourth Thursday of the month.

ENTERTAINMENT AND NIGHTLIFE
The phenomenon of the historical **son et
lumière** (sound and light) shows was created
in the Loire Valley at Chambord in 1952 and
has since gone around the world. These
grand re-enactments of each château's
colourful, often turbulent history, are
performed with costumed artists, brilliant

*Château de
Chambord at night.*

lighting effects, fireworks, illuminated fountains and music. Lasers and other modern techniques are borrowed from cinema's special effects technology, projected onto the castle façades, dramatically highlighting their architectural beauty.

Among the most spectacular are **Amboise**, where 400 local citizens perform a splendid pageant; and **Blois**, a technically avant-garde show using commentaries recorded by France's leading actors. Others include **Azay-le-Rideau**, **Chenonceau**, **Cheverny**, **Le Lude**, **Valençay** and **Loches**.

Throughout the summer, the valley is also alive with jazz, classical music, theatre and dance festivals, while Saumur stages its equestrian shows (*see* p.90).

SPORTS

If the barges plying the region's rivers move at too slow a pace, you might consider a **kayak canoe** on one of the Loire's tributaries, notably the Indre, Loir, Thouet and Vienne. Tourist offices can provide information on hiring equipment.

Horse-riding is a popular way of getting around the valley. Again tourist offices are useful sources of information on trails and possibilities for overnight accommodation with stables. **Bicycling** is best through the peaceful Sologne and Bercé forests and, of course, along the banks of the rivers, the Loire itself and its Indre tributary. Bicycles can be rented at some railway stations (*see* p.109).

Hikers can get excellent itinerary maps and useful tips from the Comité de Touraine pour la Randonnée pédestre (Touraine Hiking Association) at the Tours

Fishing on the banks of the Mayenne.

information office. There are many long-distance footpaths in the region. The **Loire Path** (Grande Randonnée) runs along the Loire through Orléans, Russy and Chinon forests.

Pike, catfish and carp, even saltwater mullet swimming upriver from the Atlantic, offer great opportunities for **fishing** in the rivers – with the appropriate permits. You'll need to hire a flat-bottomed boat for salmon-fishing, though salmon may in some years be off-limits. **Hunting** for deer, wild boar, pheasant, partridge, duck and other water-fowl is good in the forests of Sologne, Orléans and Loches.

The region's great spectator sport is the **Le Mans 24-hour motor race** in spring (*see* p.79). Out of season, enthusiasts can try their hand on the circuits south of the city.

The Bercé Forest is a lovely quiet spot for bicycling and walking.

THE BASICS

Before You Go

Visitors entering France should have a full passport, valid to cover the period in which they will be travelling. No visa is required for members of EU countries or US and Canadian citizens, but visitors from Australia and New Zealand require an entry visa. This can be readily obtained from the French Embassies and Consulates in the home country. No vaccinations are necessary.

Getting There

Getting to France has never been easier, and now that Le Shuttle and Eurostar are officially up and running the choice is even wider for UK travellers. Eurostar runs from London via the Channel Tunnel to Paris in 3 hours, while Le Shuttle takes half an hour to cross from Folkestone to Calais. France's super-efficient railway service makes the journey quite easy.

Ferries: Several ferry companies carry cars and passengers across the Channel, with the quickest journey being between Dover and Calais. The hovercraft is even faster, crossing from Dover to Calais in just 35 minutes. Brittany Ferries offer crossings

from Portsmouth and Plymouth directly to Brittany, docking at St Malo and Roscoff. For 24-hour road information (in French only) ☎ 08 36 68 20 20.

Trains: There are high-speed trains (TGV) and coach services to France from many European cities. Coaches leave London regularly for destinations all over France. If you plan to travel in the peak summer holiday period, be sure to book well in advance.

By Air: Flights leave from all over the world for various destinations in France, including the two airports in Paris – Orly

Fishing on the Vienne river.

and Roissy-Charles-de-Gaulle – and are operated by both scheduled and charter flights. Air France and Air Inter-Europe operate connecting services from both Parisien airports to Nantes. It is also possible to fly to Nantes direct from London (with Brit Air), or from Manchester to Nantes (with Regional Airlines). Package deals are available through airports and travel agencies, including flight and coach or train link-up. Fly-drive is particularly suitable for visitors to the Loire Valley, as its many attractions are spread over some distance, and the area can be best toured by car.

Arriving

There is no limit on the importation into France of tax-paid goods bought in an EU country, provided they are for personal consumption, with the exception of alcohol and tobacco which have fixed limits governing them. Holiday-makers bringing a caravan into France for a period of less than six months are not governed by customs formalities.

A-Z

Accidents and Breakdowns

Fully comprehensive insurance is advisable for motorists in France, and motoring organisations recommend that you carry a green card, although this is no longer a legal requirement. A red warning triangle must be carried by cars towing a caravan or a trailer, in case of breakdown. While this is not compulsory for non-towing cars with hazard warning lights, it is strongly recommended.

On autoroutes there are orange emergency telephones every 2km (1.25 miles), and assistance is charged at a Government-fixed rate. Motorists can only call the police or the official breakdown service operating in that area, and not their own breakdown company. This also applies on the Paris *périphérique*.

Before leaving check with your insurance company what you should do in case of an accident. Generally, if an accident happens and nobody is hurt, a form, *Constat à l'Amiable,* should be completed with full details. This must be signed by both parties, and sent off to the relevant insurers. Where someone is injured in a road accident, contact the Ambulance Service (*Samu*) on ☎ 15. The Fire Brigade is on ☎ 18 and the Police on ☎ 17.

Accommodation see p.92

Airports see Getting There p.106

Babysitters see Children

Banks

Banks are open from 9am-4.30pm Tuesday to Friday. Smaller banks close for lunch. While most banks are closed on Saturday, some banks conduct limited transactions. Banks exchange travellers' cheques, but you will need to show your passport. For simple cash withdrawals, it is simplest to use a cash dispenser (ATM), which are located outside banks and post offices and will generally accept international credit cards. *See also* **Money**.

Bicycles

The Loire region is, in the main, quite flat. This, as well as the pleasant scenery, makes the area ideal for cycling. Tourist offices provide a list of cycle hire centres, as well as details of cycling organisations who arrange tours.

Some railway stations also offer bicycles for hire which can be returned to a different station. Details are available from the SNCF.

Cyclists may also want to bring their own bicycles. Ferries and many trains will carry them free, but be warned: although cycle repair shops are common, British spare parts are scarce.

Further details of cycling in the area are available from Fédération Française de Cyclotourisme, 8 Rue Jean-Marie-Jégo, 75013 Paris, ☎ **01 44 16 88 88.**

Books

Here are a few suggestions for reading to enhance your stay in the Loire Valley:
Honoré de Balzac, *Eugénie Grandet, Le Lys dans la Vallée*
René Benjamin, *La Vie Tourangelle*
Henri-Alban Alain-Fournier, *Le Grand Meaulnes*

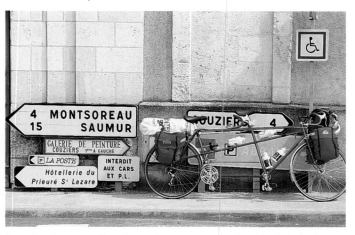

A tandem is an excellent form of transport to explore the Loire Valley.

Maurice Genevoix, *Raboliot*
Charles Péguy, *Jeanne d'Arc*
Marcel Proust, *A la Recherche du Temps Perdu*
François Rabelais, *Gargantua and Pantagruel*
Marina Warner, *Joan of Arc*
Émile Zola, *Earth*

Breakdowns see **Accidents**

Buses see **Transport**

Camping

The French are very keen campers, and the country has many efficiently run sites offering a whole range of facilities. Some campsites offer fully-equipped and permanently sited mobile homes and family-sized tents. Details of these can usually be obtained through a travel agent or specialist company.

Touring sites are very professionally organised, and you can choose from simple, basic sites in rural areas or large complexes with swimming pools, restaurants and entertainment. For full details of French sites see *Michelin Camping Caravaning France*, or apply to Féderation Française de Camping et de Caravaning, 78 Rue de Rivoli, 75004 Paris, ☎ 01 42 72 84 08.

Canal Trips see **Excursions**

Car Hire

The Loire Valley is well stocked with car-hire agencies, with outlets at air terminals and railway stations, as well as in all large towns. Airlines and tour operators offer fly/drive arrangements, and car hire in conjunction with train travel is one of the services available from French Railways.

Weekly rates with unlimited mileage offer the best deal. These include collision damage waiver, personal accident insurance and local tax, and can be booked from any country. It is worthwhile booking well in advance, and shopping around first, as there are some good deals to be had. The minimum age limit is 18, but few international companies hire to drivers under 20–23.

Drivers must have held their full licence for at least a year, and an international driving licence is sometimes required for non-EU nationals. With the exception of Avis, the maximum age limit is 60–65. Unless paying by credit card a substantial cash deposit is required, but full details of the different hire offers can be obtained from tourist offices. *See also* **Accidents and Breakdowns** and **Tourist Information Offices**.

Children

The Loire Valley is full of things to keep children occupied. It is obviously worth visiting at least one of the many fascinating châteaux for which the area is famed, but there are lots of other activities to consider.

Museums are in good supply. The Musée European de la Communication near Angers, which is actually based in Château de Pignerolle, takes the history of long-distance communications as its theme, and the Musée de la Sorcellerie at Blancafort is full of magic for imaginative youngsters. There are also transport museums at Azay-le-Rideau and Briare.

There are animal reserves too, including an excellent zoo at Doué-la-Fontaine and Bisonland at Les Cerqueux-sous-Passavant, 25km (15 miles) south of Angers.

Saumur sits peacefully by the Loire.

Children are welcome at hotels, and can share their parents' room free of charge in some hotels belonging to large chains. Restaurants in France generally cater for children, some providing special *menus pour enfants*, and the staff are often quite helpful. However, some of the more exclusive restaurants do insist that children remain seated throughout the meal. High chairs are uncommon.

Disposable nappies, baby milk products and convenience baby foods are readily available everywhere.

Churches see Religion

Climate see p.90

Clothing

The French are renowned for their sense of style. However, comfortable and casual clothes are fine for most situations, even in restaurants and theatres.

The policy regarding ties is very relaxed, although it might be wise to carry one if you are going to one of the more exclusive restaurants.

Most French clothing measurements are standard throughout Europe but differ from those in the UK and the US.

Dress Sizes

UK	8	10	12	14	16	18
France	36	38	40	42	44	46
US	6	8	10	12	14	16

Men's Suits

UK/US	36	38	40	42	44	46
France	46	48	50	52	54	56

Men's Shirts

UK/US	14	14.5	15	15.5	16	16.5	17
France	36	37	38	39/40	41	42	43

Men's Shoes

UK	7	7.5	8.5	9.5		10.5	11
France	41	42	43	44		45	46
US	8	8.5	9.5	10.5		11.5	12

Women's Shoes

UK	4.5	5	5.5	6		6.5	7
France	37	38	38	39		39	40
US	6	6.5	7	7.5		8	8.5

Consulates

Embassies and consulates can be found at the following addresses:

American Consulate 2 Rue St-Florentin, 75008 Paris
☎ 01 42 96 14 88

Australian Embassy and Consulate
4 Rue Jean-Rey, 75015 Paris
☎ 01 40 59 33 00

British Embassy
35 Rue du Faubourg St-Honoré, 75008 Paris
☎ 01 42 66 91 42

British Consulate
16 Rue d'Anjou, 75008 Paris
☎ 01 42 66 06 68

Canadian Embassy
35 Avenue Montaigne,
75008 Paris
☎ 01 44 43 29 00

Irish Embassy
4 Rue Rude, 75016 Paris
☎ 01 45 00 20 87

New Zealand Embassy
7 ter Rue Léonard-de-Vinci,
75016 Paris
☎ 01 45 00 24 11

Crime

Being the victim of theft can
ruin a holiday, so take every
precaution to prevent this
happening to you. The best
advice is to be aware at all
times, carry as little money and
as few credit cards as possible,
and leave any valuables in the
hotel safe. Never leave your car
unlocked, and hide away or
remove items of value.

If you have anything stolen,
report it immediately to the
nearest police station (*Commis-
sariat de Police*), and collect a
report so that you can make an
insurance claim. If your passport is stolen, report it to the
Consulate or Embassy at once.

Currency *see* **Money**

Customs and Entry
Regulations *see* **Arriving**
p.107

The Old Quarter of Tours.

Disabled Visitors

The *Michelin Red Guide France*
and *Michelin Camping Caravaning France* indicate which
hotels, camp sites and tourist
attractions have facilities for
disabled visitors. You can also
get information (in French)
on Minitel 3615 HANDITEL.

In Britain, RADAR, at 12 City
Forum, 250 City Road, London

EC1V 8AF ☎ 0171 250 3222, publishes factsheets as well as an annual guide to facilities and accommodation overseas. You are advised to check facilities available at hotels and at sights you plan to visit in advance. The tourist office will be able to give you up-to-date advice, (*see* **Tourist Information Offices**). Local advice centres for disabled people, run by the Association des Paralysées de France (APF), can be found at the following addresses in the Loire Valley:

Eure-et-Loire
84 Avenue Maunoury,
28002 Chartres
☎ 02 37 28 61 43

Indre-et-Loire
72 Rue Walvein, BP 0914,
37009 Tours
☎ 02 47 37 60 00

Loir-et-Cher
1 Rue Arago, 41007 Blois
☎ 02 54 43 04 05

Loire-Atlantique
1 Place Léo-Lagrange, BPP 65,
44814 St- Herblain Cedex
☎ 02 40 43 64 85

Loiret
9-11 Rue Robert-le- Pieux,
45000 Orléans
☎ 02 38 43 28 53

Maine-et-Loire
22A Boulevard des Deux-Croix, 49100 Angers
☎ 02 41 34 81 34

Mayenne
13-15 Place St-Tugal,
53000 Laval
☎ 02 43 53 25 49

Sarthe
37 Avenue de Roustov-sur-Don,
BP 207, 72005 Le Mans Cedex
☎ 02 43 28 68 46

Driving

Drivers in France should carry a full national driving licence if they are EU citizens, or an international driving licence if they are not, as well as insurance documents including a green card (no longer compulsory for EU members but strongly recommended), registration papers for the car, and a nationality sticker for the rear of the car.

Headlight beams should be adjusted for right-hand drive, and you should have a spare set of light bulbs. Full or dipped headlights should be used at night or in poor visibility.

The minimum age for driving in France is 18, and driving is on the right-hand side of the road.

Front-seat passengers must wear seatbelts, and back-seat

passengers must wear them where they are fitted. Children under ten must travel in the rear of the car.

Some traffic regulations are particular to France, eg. vehicles joining a road from the right have priority on all roads except those with a yellow diamond sign.

Those driving or speeding with a blood-alcohol level over the legal maximum (0.5g/litre) can be dealt with harshly, usually by on-the-spot fines.

Speed limits are as follows:
Built-up areas 50kph/31mph
Dual carriageways and motorways without tolls 110kph/68mph (if raining 100kph/62mph)
Toll motorways 130kph/80mph (if raining 110kph/68mph)
Other roads 90kph/56mph (if raining 80kph/50mph)
Minimum speed limit on outside lane of motorways in good conditions 80kph/50mph
For 24-hour road and route-planning information (in French) ☎ 08 36 68 20 00 or

see *Michelin on the Net* under **Maps**. *See also* **Accidents and Breakdowns**

Electric Current
The voltage in France – including on campsites – is usually 220V. Plugs and sockets vary greatly, though, and adaptors are generally required.

Embassies *see* Consulates

Emergencies
For an emergency requiring:
Police ☎ 17
Fire Brigade ☎ 18
Ambulance (Samu) ☎ 15
In some cases of emergency the Consulate or Embassy might offer limited help.
See **Consulates**

Etiquette
As in most places in the world, it is considered polite and respectful to cover up decently in churches, museums, theatres etc. The French are a more formal people than the British or North Americans. It is customary for them to shake hands when they meet and to address people correctly by their title when they are not over familiar. Thus 'Bonjour Madame/Monsieur' should begin any conversation with a shopkeeper, post office clerk or hotel desk staff, etc.

Excursions

The scenery in the Loire Valley is unparalleled. The area is well-known throughout the world for its beautiful châteaux, and the expanses of rolling countryside with its abundance of wildlife makes this an ideal destination for nature-lovers. Walking, cycling and pony trekking are popular options. It is possible to gain a bird's eye view from a small aircraft, helicopter or hot air balloon.

You can also ride on an old steam train, take a canal trip, or go down one of the many rivers on a *bateau-mouche* (some of which offer commentaries on the local wildlife), or the more adventurous could hire a canoe.

Anjou has a host of windmills which are worth a visit. It is also a flourishing wine-production area. Frequent wine fairs or feasts are held here and in the Touraine region.

Full details of these and many other tours and excursions are available from tourist offices (*see* **Tourist Information Offices**). Also refer to the *Michelin Green Guide Châteaux of the Loire* for full details of the towns, sights and attractions in the region.

Guidebooks *see* Maps

Health

UK nationals should carry a Form E111 (available from post offices) which is produced by the Department of Health, and entitles the holder to free urgent treatment for accident or illness in EU countries. The treatment will have to be paid for in the first instance, but can be reclaimed later. All foreign nationals are advised to take out comprehensive insurance cover, and to keep any bills, receipts and invoices to support any claim.

Lists of doctors can be obtained from hotels, chemists or police stations, and first aid and medical advice is also available at pharmacies (look out for the green cross). The latter are generally open from 2-7.30pm, Monday, 9am-7.30pm, Tuesday to Saturday, and those which are open late or on Sundays display notices on their doors.

Information *see* Tourist Information Offices

Language

Although English may be spoken more widely nowadays, you should not assume you will be understood if you ask a question in English. It is a

Good morning / Bonjour
Goodbye / Au revoir
Yes/no / Oui/non
Please/thank you / S'il vous plaît/merci
Sorry / Pardon
Do you speak English? / Parlez-vous anglais?
I want to buy / Je voudrais acheter
How much is it? / Quel est le prix?/C'est combien?
The bill, please / L'addition, s'il vous plaît
I'd like a booklet of bus or metro tickets / Je voudrais un carnet
Is service included? / Le service est-il compris?
Black espresso / Un café
White coffee / Un café au lait/crème
Fresh lemon or orange juice / Un citron pressé ou une orange pressée
A bottled beer / Une bouteille de bière
A draught beer / Une bière pression

good idea to take a crash course or a refresher course in the language before going to France. Whatever the level of your French, your efforts will be much appreciated, and even a few simple expressions are often warmly received.

Above is a list of some words and phrases which will help you to make the most of your stay.

Laundry

Self-service, coin-operated launderettes can be found in tourist resorts, towns and cities throughout the Loire Valley. Some of the campsites have their own. Chain dry cleaners offer a quick and cheap service, but are not always recommended for delicate clothes. Many hotels provide a laundry and dry-cleaning service.

Lost Property

Airports and major railway stations have their own lost property offices (*Bureaux des Objets trouvés*), and if something goes missing in your hotel check with the front desk and hotel security. Report all lost or stolen items to the police, and always be sure to get a report to substantiate any insurance claims.

Should you lose any travel

documents, or your passport is lost or stolen contact the police and inform your Embassy or Consulate immediately (*see* **Consulates**).

Report lost or stolen travellers' cheques and credit cards immediately to the issuing company with a list of numbers, and also inform the police.

Maps

Michelin produce a complete range of maps for the traveller in the Loire Valley. *Regional Maps* Nos. 232, 237 and 238 cover the area, but Nos. 60, 63, 64, 65 and 67 are more detailed. The *Michelin Green Guide Châteaux of the Loire* contains full information on the sights and attractions of the region.

Michelin on the Net
www.michelin-travel.com
Our route-planning service covers all of Europe. Options which allow you to choose a route are updated three times weekly, integrating on-going road-works, etc. Descriptions include distances and travelling times between towns, selected hotels and restuarants.

Money

The French unit of currency is the franc (F), which is divided into 100 centimes (c). Bank notes are issued in denomina-

tions of 500F, 200F, 100F, 50F and 20F, while coins come in 20F, 10F, 5F, 2F, 1F and 50c (all silver except the 20F and 10F coins which have a bronze border), and the bronze-coloured 20c, 10c and 5c coins.

There are no restrictions on the amount of currency you can take into France, but the safest way to carry large amounts of money is in travellers' cheques which are widely accepted and exchanged. Bureaux de change and cash dispensers (ATM) are found at airports, terminals and larger railway stations, banks and post offices (*see* **Banks**).

Exchange rates vary, so it pays to shop around. American Express, Carte Bleue (Visa/Barclaycard), Diners Club and Eurocard (Mastercard/Access) are widely accepted in shops, hotels and restaurants, motorways, petrol stations and many hypermarkets. Always check the amount which appears on the receipt, note that in France a comma is used instead of a decimal point between francs and centimes.

For information on what to do about lost or stolen travellers' cheques or credit cards, *see* **Lost Property**.

Newspapers

You can buy English language newspapers at news kiosks,

bookshops and drugstores. French daily newspapers include *Le Monde* and *Le Figaro*, and for local news *La Nouvelle République du Centre Ouest*.

Opening Hours

Shops: Department stores and larger shops usually open from 9am-6 30/7.30pm Monday to Saturday. Some food shops open on Sunday mornings – bakers, for example – and close on Mondays, and they may close from noon-2pm for lunch. Opening hours are usually 7am-6.30pm, while supermarkets stay open until 9pm/10pm.

Pharmacies: These are usually open 2-7.30pm Monday, 9am-7.30pm Tuesday to Saturday, and some open later and on Sundays. Gendarmeries will give you their addresses.

Museums and monuments: These are generally open from 10am-5pm/5.30pm, sometimes with a break for lunch. Closing day is Tuesday for national

Boating across Eiffel's canal bridge over the Loire at Briare.

museums and art galleries, and Monday for municipal museums.
See also **Banks** and **Post Offices**.

Photography

Good-quality film and camera equipment are available everywhere, and there are facilities for fast processing in larger towns.

Before taking photographs in museums and art galleries it would be wise to check with staff as photography is usually restricted in these places. In some instances hand-held cameras are admitted free, while payment is required for tripods, and flashes are forbidden.

Police

In towns and cities, French police wear a dark blue uniform and a flat cap, and are known as the *Police*, while in country areas and small towns they are *Gendarmes*, and wear blue trousers, dark blue jackets and white belts. They are all generally courteous to tourists and in emergencies can be contacted on ☎ **17**. Police can impose on-the-spot fines on drivers who violate traffic regulations.

Post Offices

Post offices are open Monday to Friday, 8am-7pm, and Saturday 8am-noon. Some are also open at other times but only offer a limited service. Stamps are also available from newsagents and tobacconists, and some hotels. Main post offices offer foreign exchange.

Air mail letters and postcards to the UK cost 3.00F, aerogrammmes, letters (under 20g) or postcards to the USA 4.40F, and letters (under 20g) to Australia and New Zealand 5.20F.

Poste restante mail should be addressed to the recipient

and sent to Poste Restante, Post Centrale, postal code of *département*, town name, France, and a passport should be taken along as proof of identity when collecting mail.

Public Holidays
New Year's Day: 1 January
Easter Sunday and Monday
 (*Pâques*)
May Day: 1 May
VE Day: 8 May
Ascension Day: 40 days after
 Easter
Whit Sunday and Monday
 (*Pentecôte*): 7th Sunday and
 Monday after Easter
France's National Day: 14 July
Assumption Day: 15 August
All Saints' Day (*Toussaint*):
 1 November
Armistice: 11 November
Christmas Day (*Noël*): 25
 December

Religion
France is largely a Roman-Catholic country, with the other major religions often represented in larger towns and cities. For particular details of churches, chapels, synagogues, mosques etc. enquire at any tourist office (*see* **Tourist Information Offices**).

Smoking
Tabacs, the licensed tobacco-nists displaying red diamond-shaped signs, sell cigarettes and pipe tobacco, but these are also on sale at certain restaurants and bars. French brands like Gauloises cost between 10–13F, while English and American cigarettes are more expensive, at 15–20F.

Telephones
Most public telephones take phonecards (*télécartes*) which can be bought from post offices, tobacconists, news-agents, and at outlets advertised on telephone booths. Cards cost around 50F for 50 units, and around 100F for 120 units.

All Paris numbers begin with **01**, those in the North-West begin with **02**, in the North-East with **03**, in the South-East with **04**, and in the South-West with **05**.

Calling abroad from France, first dial **00**, then dial **44** plus STD code (minus the first **0**)

followed by the number for the UK, **61** for Australia, **1** for Canada and the USA, **64** for New Zealand and **353** for Eire.

Cheap rates with up to 65 per cent extra time are between 9pm-8am, Monday to Friday, and at weekends from noon on Saturdays. Calls can be received at phone boxes which show the blue bell sign. For the operator ☎ **13**; for Directory Enquiries ☎ **12**; for international enquiries ☎ **00 33 12** plus country code
Emergency numbers
Fire ☎ **18**; Police ☎ **17**; Ambulance (*Samu*) ☎ **15**.

Time Difference
French standard time is GMT plus one hour. French summer time begins on the last Sunday in March at 2am when the clocks go forward an hour (the same day as British Summer Time), and ends on the last Sunday in September at 3am when the clocks go back (one month before BST ends).

Tipping
In France a 15 per cent service charge is usually included in the bill at hotels and restaurants, so there is no need to leave a tip; if you pay by cash it is considered polite to leave the small change for the waiter.

Public lavatory attendants with saucers will be happy with a few coins, but sometimes the price is displayed and is not negotiable. Tipping of 15 per cent is normal for taxi drivers, but not obligatory. There is no tipping in theatres, but cinema ushers usually expect 1F per person.

A loose guide for tipping is: Hotel porter, per bag 5F. Hotel maid, per week 50–100F. Lavatory attendant 4F.

Toilets
Public conveniences can be found at railway and bus stations, in public buildings and in department stores.

Tourist Information Offices
The French Government Tourist Office is an excellent first source of information on everything from where to stay, to what to do on wet days.

Offices are at the following addresses:
Australia BNP Building, 12 Castlereagh Street, Sydney, NSW 2000
☎ **612 231 5244**
Canada 1981 Avenue McGill College, Suite 490, Esso Tower, Montreal, PQ H3A 2W9
☎ **514 288 4264**
30 St Patrick's Street, Suite 700, Toronto, ONT M5T 3A3
☎ **416 593 4723**
Eire 38 Lower Abbey Street,

Dublin 1
☎ **1703 4046**
UK Maison de la France, 178 Piccadilly, London W1V 0AL
☎ **0891 244123**
USA France On Call Hotline:
☎ **900 990 0040** ($.50 per minute) for information on hotels, restaurants and transportation.
East Coast – 444 Madison Ave, New York, NY 10020-10022
☎ **212 838 7800**
Mid West – 676 North Michigan Avenue, Suite 3360, Chicago, IL 60611
☎ **312 751 7800**
West Coast – 9454 Wilshire Boulevard, Suite 715 Beverly Hills, CA 90212
☎ **310 271 2693**.

Local tourist offices (Comité Départemental de Tourisme) can be found at the addresses below. Those marked with an * also contain an office for Service Loisirs Accueil (*see* **Accommodation**):
Cher 5 Rue Séraucourt, 18000 Bourges

A richly-coloured tapestry depicting the Abduction of Helen hangs in the armoury at Cheverny.

☎ 02 48 67 00 18
Fax 02 48 67 01 44
*Eure-et-Loire 10 Rue du
Docteur Maunoury, BP 67,
28002 Chartres Cedex
☎ 02 37 84 01 00
Fax 02 37 36 36 39
Indre 1 Rue Saint-Martin,
BP141, 36003 Châteauroux
Cedex
☎ 02 54 07 36 36
Fax 02 54 22 31 21

*Indre-et-Loire 9 Rue Buffon,
BP 3217, 37032 Tours Cedex
☎ 02 47 31 42 53
Fax 02 47 31 42 76
*Loir-et-Cher 5 Rue de la
Voûte du Château, BP 149,
41005 Blois Cedex
☎ 02 54 78 55 50
Fax 02 54 74 81 79
Loiret 8 Rue d'Escures, 45000
Orléans
☎ 02 38 78 04 04
Fax 02 38 77 04 12
Maine-et-Loire 11 Place du
President-Kennedy. BP 2147,
49021 Angers Cedex 02
☎ 02 41 23 51 51
Fax 02 41 88 36 77
*Mayenne 84 Avenue Robert-
Buron, BP 1429, 53014 Laval
☎ 02 43 53 58 82
Fax 02 43 67 11 20
Orne 88 Rue St-Blaise, BP 50,
61002 Alençon Cedex
☎ 02 33 28 88 71
Fax 02 33 29 81 60
Sarthe 2 Rue des Maillets,
72072 Le Mans
☎ 02 43 81 72 72
Fax 02 43 82 06 64

Tourist information centres
(*Offices de tourisme/Syndicats
d'Initiative*) can also be found
in most large towns, and they
are well stocked with leaflets
providing information on
excursions, transport, entertainment, facilities for the
disabled, exhibitions, accommodation and restaurants.

The drawbridge at Chenonceau.

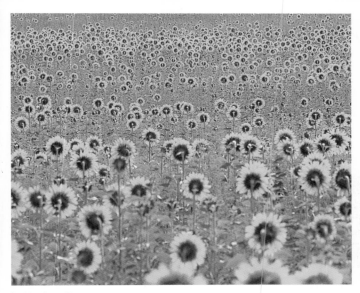

Field of sunflowers.

Transport

The French railway system (SNCF) operates an extensive network throughout France, including many high-speed trains (TGV) and motorail services. There are so many different ways of buying reduced-price tickets that you should enquire at the Government French Tourist Office in your own country for details before travelling, or at the tourist information centres or SNCF offices in France.

The SNCF also run bus services between railway stations and the surrounding areas. Most larger towns have a bus service, and you will find that many country areas have a reasonable, if infrequent, service.

There are taxi ranks (*station de taxis*) outside railway stations and in town centres. Taxis can also be hailed in the street, or you can order one by telephone.

TV and Radio

Some French hotels have TV lounges, and some have TVs in the bedrooms. All programmes

Boats on Angers' waterfront.

– apart from a few late-night ones – are in French, but English programmes are broadcast on the radio in summer, and BBC stations can be picked up easily. The BBC World Service is at at 648 long-wave and Radio 4 is at 198.

Vaccinations
see **Before You Go p.106**

Youth Hostels see **p.93**

Water
Water served in hotels and restaurants is perfectly safe to drink, as is tap water unless labelled *eau non potable* (not drinking water).

If you ask for water with a meal you will generally be given a carafe of tap-water unless you specify *eau minérale*, either *gazeuse* (sparkling) or non *gazeuse*.

INDEX

INDEX